1

2020 by Ebury Press, an imprint of Ebury Publishing,
20 Vauxhall Bridge Road,
London SW1V 2SA

part of the Penguin Random House group of companies
sses can be found at global.penguinrandomhouse.com

Penguin
Random House
UK

irst published by Ebury Press in 2020

www.penguin.co.uk

cord for this book is available from the British Library

ISBN 9781529107098

eset in 14/18 pt Garamond MT Std
Software Services Pvt. Ltd, Pondicherry

d in Great Britain by Clays Ltd, Elcograf S.p.A.

Random House is committed to a sustainable future for
iness, our readers and our planet. This book is made from
Stewardship Council® certified paper.

MA

How a ma
Br

Published i

Ebury Press is
whose addre

Dale Vince has
Work in accorda

F

A CIP catalogue re

Ty
by Integ

Printed and bou

Pengu
our bu
Forest

I'd like to dedicate this book to eco warriors everywhere – past, present and future.

CONTENTS

CHAPTER 1
CRISIS? WHICH CRISIS?

I've been bothered by the unsustainability of life since I was a kid. That's been with me all my life.

We've reached a place where modern life is the cause of so many problems; the climate crisis may be the best known, the extinction of wildlife less so – but in geological terms it's a big deal, the sixth great extinction event on our planet.

The virus crisis (aka COVID-19) is the latest and most well-known issue – it's right in our faces. It might be a surprise to hear, but this is manmade – not the virus itself; I'm not a conspiracy nut, I'm an eco nut.

Factory farming is the root cause of zoonotic viruses (like this one), those that travel from animals to humans. There are plenty in existence already and three-quarters of them come directly from animal farming; the rest are from the consequences of animal farming, like land clearance. This is a fact.

The virus spread around the world at breakneck speed, not just because it's virulent, but because of the amount of flying we do and our reluctance to shut the industry down. The record speed of contagion was caused by the record level of flying.

The virus was made more potent, infected more people and killed more people because of the air pollution we cause by burning fossil fuels. Our diets made the virus more potent too, being overweight is one of the biggest risk factors, increasing the risk of hospitalisation, intensive care and death.[1] These are all facts.

And, perhaps ironically, the virus can be carried on larger, more mobile particles of air pollution – it's hitching a ride like a passenger on a plane.[2]

These three areas of life – how we power ourselves, how we travel and what we eat – are also the fundamental drivers of the climate crisis, human health crisis and wildlife extinction.

So, we're in a place where we can solve multiple crises at the same time, with the same simple steps. I say simple – they are simple to say – just more challenging to implement. But we have the choice.

If we stop using fossil fuels and stop eating animals we can unwind all the overlapping crises that threaten to engulf us.

Modern life is without respect for nature or the value of anything, perhaps other than money. We pump pollution into the air and sea as if we think it will magically disappear, and for a while it kinda did. But seven billion of us doing this has made it noticeable.

We need to evolve the way we live so that it's within planetary boundaries – within the scope of what our planet can sustain. Everything we need and all we can ever have is on this planet. If we don't balance things up then ultimately we won't be a species this planet supports. It's a simple big picture. We're at the boundaries now. We have to evolve or die.

But it's not all doom and gloom, by any means. I'm not, this book is not.

I've spent my life in pursuit of a different way to live.

This book is about my journey, the discoveries, the experiences and real-world application of the very basic ideas that are at the heart of what's evolved into a plan: my manifesto if you like, road-tested and born of life as I've lived it.

The stuff I've been pursuing, have believed in all my life, has become technologically and economically possible, and existentially imperative. That's rather cool from my perspective.

I got lucky.

When I was a kid I wanted to travel in space, be an astronaut. Aged nine or ten I was massively disappointed to realise that I'd been born too soon, that space travel would not be common in my lifetime. My concerns about life and sustainability could just as easily have been too soon, but they've crystallised at this point in time. And I'm an econaut instead – fully fledged. This is my mission.

When you read this story it might look like I've been lucky or I'm good at spotting trends 10 or 20 years early. But I live with an innate concern for things to be sustainable so I've simply seen the things that need changing. And my nature has been to pursue that, come what may. It just so happened the world moved this way.

The course of my life has been accidental in terms of business success too, although deliberate in terms of using business as a tool and a means to be a catalyst for change. If that's a bit confusing now, hopefully it will become clear over the next few chapters.

This virus crisis has been an opportunity, it's shown us two things: we can afford to fight the climate crisis and we can make the changes we need to the way we live.

In just a few months of 2020, we committed £330 billion to the virus crisis – that's ten years of a zero carbon budget for the whole country.[3] And we endured enormous changes to the way we live, far more than those we need in order to live more sustainably.

This has reminded us of what we can do when we have a common cause and we see something as an imminent and existential threat. We need to see the climate crisis this way. There is of course no vaccine for the climate crisis and no amount of social distancing will save us.

During the virus crisis, in Britain we acted with common cause in a way and to a degree not seen since the last world war. With a fraction of this intent, we can rebuild our economy in a new way, repurpose it to tackle the fundamental drivers of climate change, wildlife extinction, poor health and social inequality. We have the chance to create a new system, rooted in sustainability in the widest sense of the word. The National Health Service was born out of the last great common endeavour of Britons; a green economy could spring from this one hand-in-hand with a new Industrial Revolution.

We need to rebuild our economy anyway; it makes sense to build a new one. The green economy that we need.

The economic benefits will be profound. The jobs and industries we create will be genuinely sustainable. We can detach ourselves from the global fossil markets and price volatility. Our economy will be stronger, more stable and sustainable. We can clean up the air that we breathe, improve lives and reduce health costs. We have the technology and natural resources to do this. And we have the need.

I've been on this journey, lived it and created businesses in all three aspects: Energy, Food and Transport. I've scoped out the technology, the scalability, and road-tested it all.

It all adds up to another way to live. Read on if you care.

CHAPTER 2
ENEMY OF THE STATE

'These Romans are crazy.'
– Obelix, friend of Asterix the Gaul

The cops came with a simple plan: violence.

It was the same plan from the same cops that had trashed the miners under orders from Thatcher in the mid eighties. Now they were coming for our convoy and the whole counterculture/new age traveller movement – call it what you will. They were pumped up, sweating buckets in full riot gear, banging long wooden sticks on their shields, like a mad modern Roman army and we were the ancient Britons. They faced off against us, a tribe of barefoot, unarmed men, women and children, and made no distinction. We were all the enemy to them. They came to break us, our homes and our way of life.

This was the Battle of the Beanfield in 1985; a wake-up call to a brutal alternative reality – one where the state saw you as an enemy. An existential threat, to be subdued by any means. I'd lived on the road through the previous summer and winter, witnessing our 'outlaw' status in practice. Being treated as criminals – on sight – as people with no rights. Initially it was the odd copper, not all by any means, but it ramped up leading to this. This was something else – the full force of the state was coming down upon us.

Many years later I found out the orders for this had come from the top of government. Margaret Thatcher saw the traveller movement as a threat, she saw us alongside the unions and the IRA – the speech she never got the chance to give to the Tory conference in Brighton (the one that was bombed by the IRA) named all three and made that clear.

The government was going to stop us at all costs. We kind of knew that but not just how far they would go. All winter long the police had been telling us not to go to Stonehenge. The site caretakers, English Heritage, had taken out a High Court injunction against persons unknown and we were up against the newly minted Public Order Act – which prevented any kind of grouping the police didn't like. But we didn't expect this.

The traveller scene had been growing through the mid eighties into a cultural movement. This was the world I went looking for in the early 1980s, when I first hit the road with my son Dane – he was about 18 months old at the time. It was a world of free festivals, of living outside (literally) and beyond normal boundaries. We lived without houses and rent and bills and all those things that either force you to have a job or force you to live in poverty, or both. This alternative culture was a melting pot of ideas, some wild and whacky, some just ahead of their time – on the fringe then, but not now. It was formed of people striking out to do their own thing, looking for another way to live, but it seemed to shock and scare the mainstream and, as often as not, inspire anger and hatred.

It was a world of new ideas; radical ways to live, non-violent protest, self-determination, sustainability, green energy, animal rights and social justice, and it was here I learned of things like the perils of the modern food industry, chemical-based agriculture and processed food pumped up with salt, sugar and fat. It hasn't changed.

We were freewheeling dropouts and mavericks, rebels with a cause and, I reckon, something of an ideology. The eighties were an austere and brutal period in the UK – it was Peak Thatcher, she won every election and brought radical, harsh policies to bear on the country. She infamously once said there is no such thing as society, and she did her best to make it so.

Years later, in 2013, I celebrated like so many others the day the wicked witch died. I didn't buy the record ('Ding-Dong! The Witch Is Dead'), but was happy to see it briefly at the top of the charts – before it got censored.

It was no wonder that so many people had drifted on to the road, whether through poverty or state violence or systemic marginalisation. The new radical dispossessed found themselves with arguably little choice but to live beyond the law, and a freethinking, live-and-let-live philosophy bound us to create a culture way beyond the mainstream.

But we had grown to be a threat and having broken the miners we were now public enemy number one, tabloid bad guys, and in the winter of 1984 they tried to break us. They pushed us from one site to another. Often (to our great amusement) the cops just pushed us over the county line and wouldn't tell the next force what was coming. It was like a game of pass the parcel. They chased us off old airfields, gravel pits, car parks and even places we would usually have permission to be – there were some. There was nowhere we were allowed to be. Our lifestyle was outside of the law.

But before they tried to break us, they made us, with a rather pointless though very civil eviction.

At Molesworth, Cambridgeshire, in the winter of 1984 they turned a peaceful occupation of an old RAF base into a 100-vehicle convoy. A convoy which was only ever going to go to one place come the spring: Stonehenge, aka the Stones.

It might have been in the summer of that year too when the festival scene and the travelling lifestyle really caught the attention of the authorities, the media and, through them, the public. *The Sun* ran regular stories about the convoy, the 'medieval brigands' fighting the police, hyping up all the worst aspects they could imagine. They are pretty good at that.

The police had come down hard on a protest at Boscombe Down airfield near Stonehenge that year. At Nostell Priory near Wakefield, riot police, fresh from trashing striking miners at Orgreave, raided a licensed festival and arrested 300 people.

I heard stories of that, of the mad cop violence, from some of the refugees that arrived at Molesworth during my stay. Molesworth was a disused Second World War airbase that the US had earmarked for siting their nuclear cruise missiles so a collective of people occupied it, setting up the Rainbow Village. It was a magical place of purpose-driven collective endeavour, and of non-violent but totally in-your-face protest. This was going on at the same time as the occupation of Greenham Common.

The Rainbow Village was anti-war and anti-nuclear in its objective and had the weekend support of members of the CND (Campaign for Nuclear Disarmament), or the Woolly Hats as they were known. They were people with jobs and stuff who would come down at the weekends to support us, bringing clothes (it was a very cold winter), food and their bodies for any protests that might happen. The village had a massive structure, built in the centre, like a circus big top, which comprised the free food kitchen and communal space. The collective of people that lived there were a mixed bunch and initially they weren't all that happy to see us arrive in the middle of the night, but we won them over. The group got more mixed when the convoy refugees from Nostell Priory arrived a couple of months later.

When they evicted the 100 or so people that were there in February 1985, it was the largest mobilisation of British troops since the last world war. More troops than it took to take Goose Green in the Falklands, according to *The Guardian*. My first son, Dane, was barely two years old – he'd been living with me on the road since the previous summer, when I split up with his mother. He got himself on the back page of *The Guardian* that day being held by a copper at the door of our bus.

In the process of this eviction, to clear the way for nukes that never came, the government created something new and set itself on the road towards that June day in the beanfield seven miles from Stonehenge.

There were always evictions. I liked this freewheeling way of life and embraced the uncertainties but after Molesworth it got intense. Wherever we parked we had the immediate attention of the police and very little time to stay before getting moved on. I was OK with it, but some of the other guys would get a bit aggressive and wind up the cops. That seemed counterproductive to me because you would have to leave anyway and all you're going to get back is violence. Cops never back down. They do violence better than anyone. That's ultimately how they stay in control.

When they arrived for the Molesworth eviction I was tripping. It was close to midnight and I'd walked out the back of the camp, into open fields, to have a pee. It was a bright, clear, cold night, there were lots of stars. It felt magical. Even peeing felt magical. I saw headlights appear on the horizon to my left. They moved all the way around our camp like a large snake (with a lot of eyes) and then, all at the same time, they turned inward, a feat of synchronised driving. It was a spooky experience, not scary but surreal. No doubt enhanced by the tripping. Turned out it was the army surrounding the camp before the police moved in. I was briefly mesmerised, then went back into the camp to tell everyone else the exciting news … something big was going down.

Though it wasn't scary to me, some of the Nostell Priory refugees were freaking out because of what they'd experienced a few weeks before. I was coming from a different place where I hadn't experienced that yet and didn't expect the cops, let alone the army, to do things like that.

That night turned out to be completely civilised. The cops just came in and said, 'This is what's happening. You're going to leave. We'll bring you fuel.' Lack of fuel was a classic reason we used to give for not being able to leave a site during eviction, to slow things down. Smart of them.

The army came in with tankers and started filling jerry cans. I spent hours whizzing around the site in my old breakdown truck, yellow lights flashing – delivering fuel, pulling trucks out of the mud, getting engines ready – most had no cooling water as we couldn't afford antifreeze, and so drained our engines when stationary in winter. It took till the early hours to get everyone fired up and moved to the road. It was a very well-organised eviction, decently executed in an almost stereotypical English way.

Then we hit the road. They clearly had no idea what to do with us, no plan for this part, so they just pointed us towards the next county. With that eviction they created a bit of a monster, easily the biggest convoy of alternative types yet – and it eventually made its way towards Stonehenge.

In the early hours of the eviction I was stood with a friend, Steve, on the edge of our site, behind a wall of coppers and media as Michael Heseltine (the Secretary of State for Defence) arrived in a chopper, jumped out in his flak jacket and – I was close enough to see – his face heavily made-up ready for the cameras. It was a bit of a juxtaposition and another super surreal moment for me. This was how TV news was created.

One of our first stops after Molesworth was Grafham Water, a lake near Huntingdon, Cambridgeshire. The lake was frozen. I remember walking out late at night on the ice to see how far I could get. Why not, right? I was feeling a bit overconfident, looking for the edge of things (not for the first time), and once I got a long way out, with little else to do, I lifted my leg and brought it down hard on the ice. I didn't think it through, just did it. I was a long way out and there was nobody around. In response the ice just started cracking. 'Fuck' was my one-word silent reaction – and I slid my feet as quickly and gently as I could all the way back to the edge of the lake, followed by the sounds off cracking ice. It was a pretty mad thing to do – a close call, exhilarating and illuminating all at the same time. If the ice had broken I reckon I would have died that night. There was nobody there to help, if help was even possible. And nobody would have known where I went.

We got kicked off that site after a few days. I'd spent most of that running out to pick up broken-down stragglers. It was a special time. The détente of the Molesworth eviction was holding; I had no number plates or tax or anything on my truck. When I got stopped I'd just say, with causal confidence, 'Your chief constable knows what we're doing, he's OK'd it' (and he actually had on the night of the eviction). The cops would look at each other and we'd be waived on our way. Clearing the roads was a public service, for a week or two.

We moved to an old airfield next and I jumped my first police roadblock in the process. The cops had decided to try and corral us out of their area and blocked all but one road off a large roundabout. We all came to a stop, filling up the roundabout and the road we'd approached from, and had a chat about what to do about it – I'd seen the exit road we wanted had verges, big gaps their vehicles didn't fill, and when we fired back up I just drove up the kerb and bypassed them, on the verge. That broke the deadlock, the cops pulled out and let us carry on our way. I was quite elated by that experience: it was a totally non-violent act of rebellion.

We had to move again, this time pushed on by cops and angry farmers in big four-wheel-drive tractors. They got a bit carried away, ramming one of our vehicles, but the cops let it go. Back on the road again, it was clear that the cops had no idea how to handle this huge convoy of vehicles they had created. They were acting as individual forces, moving us on, not caring and not warning neighbouring forces we were coming ... Thatcher's credo perhaps: everyone for themselves.

I was driving the lead vehicle (my bus) that day and I remember we had a police escort, a Range Rover with its lights on. Our plan was to turn left and go around the back of Molesworth and try and retake the site – the cops had asked which way we were going, keen for us to go straight down the road and out of their area, and as we approached the turn off the senior cop, a passenger in our police escort, turned round, looked at me and gestured down the road in a questioning kind of way. I gestured thumbs up to confirm but, as I got there, turned hard left and the game was on. We were stopped in our tracks a mile or so later by cops blocking the road – but just past the entrance to a piece of land big enough to park on, which was their mistake. I skewed my bus across the road, just past the site, to hold the entrance for everyone else to get through. The cops were furious, but I wasn't going to move it and we took the site – but not for long.

Come spring we were in Savernake Forest in Wiltshire. It became a staging point as groups joined from all over the country. I don't know how word used to spread back then. This was way before mobile phones and social media – but it did. People came from everywhere and we all had the same intent: going to Stonehenge.

That morning a multicoloured convoy of a good couple of hundred vehicles set off, slightly anxious but with a party spirit, towards the ancient and iconic Stonehenge. It was the first of June 1985 and the convoy of living vehicles – old buses, vans, trucks, caravans, everything you could imagine – was wending its way through Wiltshire. We'd been on the national news every night as we closed in on this most iconic of ancient sites for the most iconic of annual free festivals. There was drama to come.

The cops had set up a roadblock. They planned to stop the convoy in a dead end and trash it. We were the new enemy within. We were going to feel the full force of the state and all the illegality it was capable of. Which as it turned out was a great deal.

By 1985, the Stonehenge festival was getting too big and too lawless and the travellers were national news. There'd been a free festival there since 1974. It was the early 1980s when I bumped into it. The festivals were just amazing – wild and free – a place where you could do what you wanted, a world of sound systems and bands, of magic mushrooms and hot knives (a cannabis thing) in the makeshift cafés, of community and a common cause. I loved it. It was anarchic in the true sense but at times violent, for people that had those tendencies – a bit like life more generally.

In 1985 there was a concerted effort to prevent the festival happening. English Heritage, who 'own' the stones;

the National Trust, which owns the surrounding land; and Wiltshire County Council, which owns the highways and verges, joined forces to stop the festival with a series of High Court injunctions – against persons unknown – which seemed pretty outrageous to me. To many of us, the Stones weren't somewhere we could be told not to go, they didn't belong to English Heritage or to the government – they were everybody's.

Stonehenge has seen a lot of history. We made a little more that day.

It's an impressive place, all the more so when you consider that these huge, 4-metre-high bluestones had been dragged all the way from Wales, 150 miles across the hills, in ancient times (so, no M4) and built into this mysterious circle. It's still a mystery how they did that, and why – the most likely purpose the Stones have is to mark time, the passing of the seasons, punctuated by the extremes of the summer and winter solstice, the longest and shortest days of the year. It was one of the last great circles, built 5,000 years ago in the Neolithic period and surrounded by ancient roads, Ley lines, burial mounds and long-lost older circles. It's a place of magic, of folklore, ancient religions, enigmatic and stoic; standing through the centuries. It's arguably the heart of ancient Britain.

Yeah, the Stones have seen a lot of history. Winter and summer solstice ceremonies for sure, but what else did the Druids do there? There's so much we don't know but, and this is only a guess, few events at the Stones were as violent and one-sided as the Battle of the Beanfield. This battle of cultures that took place a few miles down the road between the ragtag band of travellers I was with and the state in full-on fascist mode.

The police plan was to let us wind our way down narrowing roads and then, miles from any turning point, surprise us with a roadblock, trap us and then attack the convoy. That plan didn't work. I was riding ahead on my motorbike that day, looking for trouble that might lie ahead, and enjoying the ride. It was a nice day and there was nothing better for me than riding. I had a Ducati 450 single cylinder, a really special bike – I still have it. I was in effect an outrider for the convoy and, as I spun around the country lanes about a mile ahead of the lead vehicle, I turned a bend and came upon the trap. It was the most serious roadblock I'd seen: three tipper trucks parked side-by-side across the road, with their backs tipped up and a wall of aggregate lying across the road and a sea of cops behind it – there were no grass verges this time, no way round. This was a roadblock that would trap the convoy in a dead end.

I did a U-turn without stopping – this bike was so well balanced I could lock the back wheel and skid around, dropping gears as I slid and shot off in the other direction. It was poetry in motion to me. It had saved me from a mob of angry Mods many years earlier in Great Yarmouth. And probably just as well. As I blasted back along the road I heard a helicopter and looked over my shoulder – there it was, chasing me down the twisting road. Back in the convoy a friend listening to the police radio heard them say 'they've got a motorcycle outrider – stop the motorcycle outrider' but there was not much a chopper could do and all the cops and all their vehicles were trapped behind their own barricade. As I hared down that road, hoping to get to the lead vehicle before the last turn away from the trap, I looked again over my shoulder at the pursuing chopper and felt I was in a James Bond film.

I got back just as the lead vehicle of the convoy was approaching the last turn off. It was being driven by Phil the Beer – he didn't like me much at that time, I would say, as we'd clashed a few times since Molesworth, just a clash of opinions of judgements, but the feelings were strong on his side – and I wasn't sure he would actually stop as I urgently flapped my arm at him. But he did and I told him what was ahead. We made a left turn, the only option we had. A few hundred metres later, we turned right at a T-junction and were now running parallel to the road we were originally on. As we were to find out through the court proceedings that eventually followed, the police scrambled from their roadblock to compensate. They ran head first into the lead vehicles, ramming them, and as the convoy stopped they ran up the line of vehicles, smashing windscreens and dragging people out if they could.

It was mad violence – total lawlessness. The first ten or so vehicles were battered and a few turned, looking for a way out, and drove clean through the hedgerow to our right, into a big empty field. As others saw this, the whole convoy did the same thing – some of us used chainsaws to make a path and within minutes most had made it to relative safety.

There were 1,300 police and 600 travellers so they certainly had the numbers; they also had the riot gear and the organisation, and they had trained for this – and practised on the miners. But this was chaos. We'd thwarted their original plan and, like a swarm of angry bees, they attacked us, with venom and spite.

All the vehicles that could make it into the field had done so and an eerie kind of calm fell on us – laced with adrenaline and dread, from what had just happened and of what they would do next. We were under no illusions – we'd just been rammed by the advance guard of the police, dashing from their blockade to prevent us getting to the main road just ahead. There weren't many at first, but they were uber violent – and we could see them organising, collecting themselves into a new battle position.

Somebody broke out a sound system, but nobody really thought this was ending in a festival. A group of travellers congregated by the main entrance into the field – to front the police. We were told to surrender and we would all be arrested (there was never any suggestion of what laws we might have broken) – and that was it: no other negotiation.

It took an hour or two for them to get themselves ready – but when they were, they charged into the field screaming and banging their shields. And smashing everything and everyone in their path. There were no attempts made to simply arrest or to do anything in a remotely peaceful fashion: it was unmitigated, indiscriminate violence.

I was living in a small ambulance that month. My bus had gone to someone that needed it more than me, and I'd put my bike in the back of this little ambulance before things started to get crazy. As the police attacked, a bunch of us jumped into vehicles and drove into the next field, it was the only place to go to get away from them – but it too was a dead end. It was a beanfield and that's where the name the Battle of the Beanfield comes from.

We couldn't find a way out. We were just going round and round this beanfield. It was here where some of the scenes of greatest violence were to be had. Because I was in a small vehicle, I didn't attract a lot of attention from the cops. They were after the larger buses: they seemed to provoke outrage among the cops – they were the focal point. I saw cops throwing rocks and truncheons and helmets at windscreens as the vehicles drove by and when they did manage to stop a bus they dragged the driver out through the broken windshield, went on board and beat everybody.

The cops were trashing everything. It was a frenzy.

I watched, more than a little horrified as I drove around, oddly able to spectate, wondering how this would end. Then a cop saw me, looked right at me and just pointed; I knew he meant me to 'stop'. So I did, the gig was up: there was nowhere to go. I got out of my ambulance and took off my bike helmet – I had some faith in this guy, I don't know why. And he was decent. An older guy, he told me to put my hands on the truck for a search. He wasn't even rough, let alone aggressive. So I was really lucky.

But while I was stood there this other cop came running over with his truncheon and actually jammed it up my backside – he was totally wired, talking shit. The decent cop stopped him, told him to leave. It was pretty impressive. I may have found the one decent cop there. I've never told this story before. I've never swapped stories of that day with anyone – I think it was more traumatic than I realised.

Years later, I met with another decent cop. A local TV company was making a documentary about the Battle of the Beanfield; it was the twentieth anniversary, I think, and they asked me to visit the site. I took my old motorbike along for the trip, that was a blast. They introduced me to this guy, a cop that was also there that day of the battle (though battle isn't really the right term). I didn't know quite what to expect, but I expected confrontation to a degree and argument – that we deserved it or at least that there were bad people on both sides or something like that – but he was really friendly, actually apologetic. That was a shock. He told me that he'd resigned from the force that day after what he had seen. He was so shocked he quit the force.

Five hundred and thirty-seven of us were arrested. It was the biggest mass arrest in the UK since the last world war. We were dispersed to cop shops all over the place because they arrested so many people and there was nowhere to put us all – it was like they hadn't thought that part through. And they drugged us. I don't know what they used, some of the other guys talked of Largactil, a drug used in prison. I had no idea but I think they put it in the water. We all just passed out on the floor – it was weird. Eventually, it might have been the next day, they let us go but left us wherever they'd taken us, with no transport or anything. Some of us had no shoes and we were 10 or 20 miles away from the Beanfield and what was left of our vehicles. Turns out our vehicles had been dragged away and smashed to bits, windows trashed and brake lines cut. The whole back end of my ambulance was just ripped off.

I ended up back at Savernake where a lot of survivors congregated. I slept outdoors that night around a fire as I didn't have a vehicle. In the morning a friend told me that I'd freaked them out by sleeping with one eye open. I slept like that for a long time afterwards, years. It had that kind of impact on me.

The guy that owned the land, the Earl of Cardigan, a distant relative to the guy that led the Charge of the Light Brigade (the press made much of that), let us stay at Savernake for a while.

He'd seen what the police had done at the Beanfield and when the cops asked him if they could 'come and finish the job' he refused. I thought that was pretty amazing, especially for an establishment figure – later I learned of his infamous quote to the British media about the Battle of the Beanfield. He said 'he had seen men born, and he'd seen men die, but he'd never seen anything like what happened on that day'.

He also said, 'If I see a policeman repeatedly truncheoning a very pregnant woman over the head from behind, as I did, I do feel I'm entitled to say "that's a terrible thing you're doing, Officer." I went along, saw a dreadful episode in British Police history, and simply reported what I saw.' How very British that sounds. The press shredded him.

His powerful statement was key many years later in our defence and nearly all the serious charges were dropped against the travellers. Mostly we were charged with criminal damage to the beans, laughable but true. It's on my rap sheet, even though driving into that field was absolutely an act of self-defence, and the actions of the police were absolutely criminal.

It was wanton state-sponsored violence and we were guilty of damaging beans while trying to avoid it ... I think the court system just had to pin something on us, despite the overwhelming evidence of police foul play.

In the weeks that followed that violent confrontation a few of us talked about leaving the country – not for the first time – and some had already left for Spain. I thought that was the best thing to do to avoid any more conflict.

But I needed a vehicle – mine was beyond repair.

I built a new one that following winter in Wales and got ready to leave the country.

CHAPTER 3
HEAD FIRST

I was suddenly aware, conscious of being. Before that I wasn't: it was like time had just started for me. My eyes were closed, this much I knew, and from within this blackness I surveyed my physical feelings and tried to make sense of everything. I had a concept of being but no idea who I was.

I told myself a joke. It amused me, but smiling hurt. I thought if I'd been in a fight I'd hate to see the other guy. It was a simple, common kind of joke. I had no idea if I had been in a fight. I had no idea of anything except the injuries I was becoming conscious of. And of being alive.

I tried to open my eyes. One of them wouldn't. It was properly closed. A nurse spotted me, seemed apprehensive or surprised, and I knew only that she was calling me by the wrong name. I was strapped to a bed in hospital. I had no memory of anything. No idea how I got there, where there was, who I was – anything.

I was 16 years old. I was a biker and I'd had a head-on collision with a car. I went head first through the windscreen and ended up inside the car. Not many people survive going through a car windscreen the conventional way (inside out) and there can't be many people unfortunate enough to do it the way I had, from outside in. I was incredibly lucky to be alive.

It was a split-second event that left a big imprint on my life.

I still have a gap in my memory from the collision to when I woke up in that hospital, apparently not my first hospital in that 24 hours. I learned later of a roadside search for missing teeth, of an ambulance trip with language more industrial than they said they'd heard before, and of my mother in that first hospital (A&E, I presume) crying and me saying, 'Don't cry – you're upsetting me.'

It doesn't sound any fun. I don't remember it, it's what I've been told.

I was strapped to a bed in Lowestoft Hospital, and later learned they don't give you painkillers when you've got potential head injuries so I'd been a bit leery – hence, perhaps, the earlier reaction from the nurse. I was in a lot of pain. My head was swollen like a football; I had a mouth full of broken or missing teeth, cracked cheekbone and jaw, broken nose, closed eye, some glass lodged in my throat and, least of all, a broken wrist. But I was conscious and amusing myself with a silly joke.

I had total amnesia, massive head injuries and a simple recollection of becoming conscious. It was like somebody had flicked on a switch. And starting like this, starting my life again, had a profound impact on me philosophically, not just physically.

Until that point I was a troubled kid, constantly clashing with my parents and any other form of authority. I'd not long left school where I struggled to fit in, to accept the rules and the order of things. Leaving school was for a long time the happiest day of my life. I thought of it like getting out of prison, getting my life back because school was almost all I'd known, it had taken my life to that point. But I had similar issues at home; control and rules, both appearing petty and arbitrary to me, pressure to conform and get a job. I was pretty unhappy – when I was at home anyway. Out on the road, on my bike and with my friends, life was very different.

But I didn't know any of this when I woke up. I was almost blissful, battered and bruised as I was, in a world I didn't understand. I was happy because I had no memories to trouble me – only the present existed.

It struck me at the time that it's memories that give you pain. If you have no memory, nothing that has gone on before can hurt you, it doesn't matter and might as well not have happened. I was experiencing a massive example of that. It wasn't just my life I couldn't remember but the accident and the aftermath, the trauma and the pain. These were (and still are) things that didn't, couldn't, affect me.

It changed the way I looked at my life and I think I became inured to the idea of death, or more comfortable with it. It made me a little more bold, perhaps crazy, or at least my friends thought so. Maybe it was the head injury.

As my memory started to come back, I went from being a beaten but happy blank canvas to being that troubled kid again. I just wanted to get out of there. My parents came in on the day I woke up, and walked straight past the bed because they didn't recognise me, and I didn't recognise them either. We were strangers. But as that changed I got restless.

I was in hospital for somewhere between one and two weeks and within days of getting out I was on the back of a friend's bike, my arm in a sling and the spare sleeve of my bike jacket in my mouth to stop it flapping in the high-speed wind. I was excited but more than a little anxious; I never enjoyed being a passenger.

This insight stayed with me: memories bring pain and distract from the here and now. I could have died in that accident, or just afterwards – somewhere in that memory gap I still have, but it wouldn't really have mattered, there would be no enduring suffering. It gave me a different way to look at life and death; It made me more fatalistic than I already was.

We interpret the world differently, all of us, and we experience it differently – but it's real to us. Memories and experience are things that we carry with us through life and they add to who we are. And the absence of memory was an amazing experience. As my memories started to come back, the unhappiness came back with them. The circumstantial unhappiness crept back in and made me want to change my life.

I'd left school, and now I needed to leave home.

CHAPTER 4
THE BUS DIARIES

My time on the road was a decade-long adventure, punctuated with different vehicles and different sites; festivals and winter park-ups – and different ways of making a living.

The Stones and the Battle of the Beanfield were a big part, so too Europe and, towards the end of that decade, Glastonbury and dabbling in renewable energy.

My first vehicle was a Bedford J Type ambulance, grey with a petrol engine – it was 30 years old if it was a day. Cost nearly nothing, was in good nick – they really don't make them like they used to – and did a remarkable amount to the gallon. The back had been converted into a camper: it was a perfect starting place. Oh and when the battery was flat, you could start it with a handle – proper old-school, and very effective.

I was living in Lowestoft at the time. It was there I decided to make the big change, broke free of an abusive relationship and hit the road. Dane, my first son, was maybe 18 months old when we left Lowestoft together in this old ambulance and went in search of a new way to live, just the two of us.

It was summer in the early eighties; we drove out of town late one night, having just acquired some petrol, with no destination, hoping to bump into what we were looking for. Which was essentially just another way to live. It was strange at first, driving and parking up, living out the back of that van – halfway in, halfway out of society.

After maybe a week or two, we found our way to the edge of Wales and the Cantlin Stone free festival. This was a proper anarchic affair, with no real start or end date, essentially a land squat on the edge of commercial forestry, and it ran into the magic mushroom season in autumn.

People came and went all summer. It was a great place to hang out and learn new life skills and meet people. It was here I met people that had witnessed the breaking of the miners' strike and the brutality of the police. And here that I first saw the Blue Lake bus, which later I would live in – it was in the hands of a proper anarchist crew then. As summer came to a close one of my new travelling friends invited me to join a small group overwintering somewhere deeper into Wales, somewhere they knew: Llangybi Common.

I started my first winter living outdoors in the woods – houseless but not homeless – and did a bit of work on an organic farm. I tried to build a teepee, having wanted to live in one since I was a kid, but only managed the poles. I learned that woods are not a good place to park in the winter; it carries on raining long after it's actually stopped because of dripping trees.

Dane's mother Kath found me there and asked if she could take him for a while. I let her but regretted that for the next ten years or more, as once she had him she made it hard for us to see each other.

I swapped my ambulance for the Blue Lake bus while at Llangybi Common and made the midwinter trip to Molesworth from there, with my teepee poles.

At Molesworth I got another Bedford J Type, red, and this time a bull-nosed pick-up truck with a breakdown crane on the back for about 50 quid. It turned out to be really useful, while I lived there, during the eviction and for a long time afterwards – it got me into towing and scrapping stuff.

By the time of the Beanfield I lived in a really small ambulance, a BMC with a little four-cylinder diesel engine, the bus and the tow truck having moved on to new owners. I could fit my Ducati in the back so it was big enough.

Next I lived in a bender with Karen; we hooked up after the Beanfield, in the Welsh border region again, at another free festival.

Benders are cool, like an English igloo, hazel poles bent into a dome shape and covered in tarpaulin – we got most of our tarps off the back of lorries. Inside we had a small stove, made from a five-gallon oil container, stood upright with a flap cut into the front with tin snips and bent back serving as a door, and a flexi-pipe chimney on top, exiting through the canvas – bit dodgy but nobody died that way as far as I know. It was a really cosy way to live, the worse the weather the more so, unless you were on ground that got sodden; for that you needed a pallet floor. Lorries had them too.

We found an old fire engine in a field not far away – just a cab and a chassis with four wheels – and managed to track down the guy who owned it. He was a bad man; we gave him the 200 quid he was asking for and he turned his back to count it to his father (so we couldn't see), then turned to us and declared it 40 quid short. It wasn't – or hadn't been until then – and his father looked embarrassed. We argued but paid the extra 40 quid so we could move on. As we were leaving the old guy tried to give us 20 quid for good luck. I told him to keep it – because money mattered more to them than it did to us.

We'd been planning to go to Spain since the Beanfield. That chassis cab was the basis of the truck we would leave the country in, and much more, but first it needed some work. It had a petrol engine, a big one this time, was four-wheel drive, had a crew cab that was big enough to live in – but had been stood in that field for years so not much was working.

We took it back to the festival and I got it more roadworthy; fixed the cab up, blocked off the missing driver-side door, sorted some lights, bolted wooden planks across the back and put a small breakdown crane on top – the crane from my old Bedford breakdown truck, which was also there. The site was getting evicted – repossessed by the bank. A friend found somewhere to park for the winter, a farm nearby, and we drove there. We slept in the barn the first night – we had nowhere else – then stitched a big blanket together, stuffed it with straw and used it as a mattress in the cab. Our new home.

This truck needed an engine transplant to be converted to diesel. I found an engine that might fit in a nearby scrapyard and negotiated a swap. I knew the petrol engine had value, the four-speed Bedford gearbox was wanted for export – that helped.

I dropped the petrol engine on to blocks and then pushed the fire engine backwards so that it came out of the front. Old lorries were great for this and four-wheel drive more so, as it was much easier to get underneath them. The scrap-yard guys came along, picked up our engine and dropped the diesel one on to the same blocks – this was my puzzle to solve now – how to get this bigger engine into the truck, avoiding the differential on the front axle (four-wheel drive) and all sorts of related issues.

I had a bottle jack, socket set and some concrete blocks. That was my toolkit. And a blacksmith's down the road. As I worked out how this would fit, lifted at the rear, twisted to one side and sticking out the front a bit, I sketched up brackets which they made for me and I took them back and forth for tweaking. The gear lever was a mare – the original wouldn't fit – so it was a stick with no gate, no guide, and you had to move it like there was one. If you messed up you had to backtrack and try to reset. It made it a truck that virtually only I could drive. Years later, when the cops tried they got stuck in first gear and got nowhere fast.

The engine was decades more modern than the truck, it was 24v while the truck was 12; I rigged two batteries with big master switches which gave me 24v for starting the thing and 12v for running it. The sequence was crucial though: one off before the other on, or serious sparks would fly.

It was a good challenge that took most of the winter. Eventually I got it in and working, so we hit the road looking for some better tyres to make the trip abroad. We found some in Bedford at a big army surplus depot. I loved that place.

A few weeks later, with my motorbike on the back, we jumped on a ferry at Dover and landed in France. The next day we had a run in with the local police as we had no number plates or anything, it was proper pirate stuff. We told them we were going to Spain, expecting this would help them see their way to just ignoring us – instead they asked how much money we had. We bluffed, told them it was a few hundred quid (it was more like 50) but they insisted on seeing it, which was awkward. We showed them, they laughed, thought it crazy and funny we were going to get to Spain in this vehicle with 50 quid – and they let us on our way. To be someone else's problem.

We spent a couple of days driving down to the Pyrenees and the border with Andorra. This truck was old, but the engine (and brakes now) were more modern. On the flat it was good for 50, and it would do that up the steepest hill, and close to it with a double decker on the back (which we did years later in Cornwall). Truckers would overtake us on the flat, an exotic annoyance to them – only to see us fly by on the next hill in this crazy, beaten-up old fire-engine breakdown truck.

Going over the Pyrenees was fun; we stopped the first night part way, still climbing upward, pulled over by the side of the road, whipped out our gas ring from under the bed at the back and made dinner in our one pot, on the engine cover. We used to whip up quite a feast this way – this was the last of our supplies from England though.

Later that night the big road sign out the windscreen started flashing *Équipement obligatoire* as the weather turned white. It was a warning in French that snow chains were obligatory going any further up the Pyrenees. Exciting stuff.

Our truck was ancient, but it was four-wheel drive and we had off-road tyres. We cruised on up the road, through Andorra and down to Spain the next day. Feeling a little cocky.

As we drove down the mountains it was like driving through the seasons, winter gave way to spring then summer. Spain was beautiful.

We drove to the south coast and then along it – no destination really, no plan – thinking we might bump into other travellers. It was an adventure.

Eventually we bumped into some types in a market as we neared Gibraltar, blagging old vegetables at the end of the day (our first lesson in survival in Spain), and we headed off to a nearby site to join a small group of English people by a river, near La Linea (The Line), the town that borders Gibraltar.

We stayed there a fair while. Did some busking and I learned to juggle; I made some clubs from a broom handle and old water bottles. Karen could play the flute – I had a guitar. It would be exaggerating to say I could play it, but I could make some noise. If someone tuned it for me, it sounded better – occasionally passers-by would offer to do this for me, which I still find amusing. I learned a couple of flamenco chords and had a homemade flamenco-sounding riff, which actually was a crowd-pleaser.

We lived that way for a while and it became like a job. We'd catch the bus to Gibraltar in the morning, set up at the entrance near the Moroccan quarter and earn enough to eat that day: the Moroccan café for pea soup and bread was the place, super-tasty, priced for migrant workers and very friendly – we even had a kick about in the yard. Then off home. And repeat.

It got old. Living in Spain actually got old. From England it appeared to be like the answer to all our hassles and maybe our dreams – good weather, cheap to live in, easy-going people and cops – but after a while it got boring.

We decided to drive on to Portugal.

Getting in wasn't easy. We bumped again into the question of how much money we had. The border cops had an entry level, you had to show the cash – without it they just wouldn't let you in. That was my first time being refused entry to a country. Not the last.

We were stumped, but some Spanish guys in a car behind saw what happened and offered to help, they gave us the cash to show the border cops and held my guitar as security (a notional idea given its actual value). Once across the border we swapped back.

Then they took us to a bar and bought us dinner. Amazing. We met some really lovely people in Spain. And in Portugal. Our first morning there we were woken by the sounds of donkeys and carts. That's how life was there, out in the sticks.

We drove south to the Algarve, again hoping to bump into travellers. By now we had nothing, and our busking didn't work. I think it was because the audience were tourists not locals – they had very little empathy.

We parked on the beach, which sounds idyllic and it was in a way – we just lacked cash. I traded an electric drill, my last thing of any value, and we ate for a couple of days. By then we'd hooked up with a local guy who did stuff like collect lost golf balls and sell them back to golfers. He took me with him. There was a deep pool on the course, with a lot of balls on the bottom. He never went for them, nobody did – not sure why. I've got big lungs, getting that deep and staying there long enough was easy enough and I plundered this store of lost balls (we got about 50p each for them). It was a good day. We subsisted that way for a while, scrumping fruit trees on the way home from golf.

While we were there my guitar was stolen; our truck didn't lock and one day someone just took it. A day or two later I was sleeping in the shade when I had one of those dreams – the ones that are about to happen in reality. I've had a few. I dreamed I saw Karen carrying my guitar away from a camp of people. I woke up as she turned up, holding it, breathless. She'd been out with our friend and bumped into a nearby Gypsy camp, she saw my guitar and, Karen being Karen, just grabbed it and took it back. Our friend stayed behind to try and smooth things. He turned up shortly after and told us to get moving, quickly – the Gypsy group were angry and were coming after us. We moved into some nearby woods and nothing came of it, but by now we were done with Portugal and we set off back into Spain.

We ended up near Gibraltar again, hooked up with some types in a bus, did some busking together and jumped on a boat one day to go to Morocco to check it out. This was my second entry refusal: they wouldn't let me off the boat because of my long hair. I went back to Spain, chopped it off and went straight back – appearances are everything it seems. I was in and Morocco was an amazing experience.

Karen went back to England and I lived on my own in Spain for a while. The people I hung out with spoke no English – which was great, really immersive. I became friends with a guy called Gato and hung out in a local beach bar. I picked up the language that way. A key moment was when I learned how to say 'how do you say that in Spanish' in Spanish. Eventually I was thinking and dreaming in Spanish, which was really cool – and with my Gypsy blood (which I did not yet know of) turned a convincing shade of local brown.

What with that and my guitar, tourists used to speak to me in broken, loud English – that was amusing. While I was there my trainers fell to pieces and I went barefoot for a while. Some guys saw me one day and were horrified, made a big fuss – one of them took me to his house and gave me a pair of his. They were lovely people.

The truck by then had an engine problem I just couldn't find – and I was a pretty ace diesel mechanic. I did all the stuff I could in Spain, to the injectors and the injector pump, but it wouldn't run properly.

I flew back to England one day on a standby ticket out of Gibraltar (aka Gib to the locals). That was my first time flying and it was exciting. Gib has a very short runway that ends at the sea; planes jam their brakes on, gun their engines, then let the brakes go – the result is big acceleration for a short distance and a rapid ascent into the air and fairground-style whirlypits in the stomach. I had the injector pump from the truck with me, thinking it was a deeper problem than I could sort in Spain, more technical than my Spanish was. But the pump was fine.

I got arrested on the return trip, not unusual, sleeping in the airport – looking suspect I suppose. They took me to court the next day; they had outstanding warrants for the Beanfield and stuff that winter, but they let me go, not sure why. But I think they thought I was up to something else and would wait for me to come back in my truck – which is exactly what happened.

Back in Spain I finally found the problem. A tiny metal piece called a 'woodruff key' had sheared, causing the injector-pump timing to slip, making the engine run all kinds of wrong, powerless and smoky … with that breakthrough I could hit the road again. But it was running rough; time had properly caught up with that old scrapyard engine that had carried us across Europe.

I decided to drive back to England. The shortest way was to drive the entire length of Spain, from Gibraltar at the very bottom to Santander in the north and then jump on the 24-hour ferry to Plymouth. That was still a long trip for this engine.

I blagged some fuel and the ferry fare, and had enough cash for a big bag of oranges from the local market. That sustained me for the trip of several days. My engine by then was knackered, using water and oil like there was no tomorrow. We limped, smoked and rattled our way across Spain and landed in England.

And got arrested again; maybe it's just the way I look, or it was the truck, or maybe they were waiting. This time the truck got impounded, searched, taken apart. I was held for about 24 hours while they did this; they found nothing, because there was nothing, then let me go. It was during this incident that the cops tried to drive my truck. After I'd been arrested they wanted to take it to a workshop – they told me later when they released me – and although they weren't that friendly before, once I was clear of suspicion they were decent guys. They told me how they'd started to drive and as they changed into second gear, or tried to, the lever slipped into no man's land and they were stuck, 5mph in first all the way. You had to know how to use that box. I had it straight in a jiffy and drove on out of there.

Back in Blighty I set out to rebuild that engine and as I opened it up it more or less fell apart – it's incredible that we made it back. The piston rings literally fell to pieces, the big and small ends and the main bearings were shot – it needed a total rebuild, but these engines are easy to do that with. I had it up and running in no time, even better than the day I first put the engine in that truck for sure.

And I was back on the road, looking for travellers, looking for work.

I spent five years living in the cab of that lorry. Put two different engines in it, three cranes on the back, did all sorts of other stuff: upgraded brakes, springs, electrics, added towing stuff, made bumpers – and I lived in it and worked with it.

Back in England, I hooked up with Karen again.

The next vehicle I bought was quite exceptional. I spotted it at Blackbushe auction. It was a 4x4 Bedford with a coach-built body, double-skinned aluminium in royal blue, had fuel and water pumps and was made for servicing choppers. The roof was low and, being 4x4, the floor was high and squeezed in the middle. You couldn't stand up in it so we would live on the floor, Japanese-style. It had an amazing vibe inside. But it had been sold already. I was undeterred – this vehicle was too amazing to give up on.

Only three were ever made, for the Queen's Flight, and some guy bought them all for export but they couldn't start this one and it got left behind. I got his phone number from the auctioneers and offered him 500 quid for it – he went for it, which was amazing. The auction people told me he'd paid three times that. I got lucky; he'd just got back from holiday, had exported the first two, probably for a very decent price, and I was offering to take this problem one off his hands – it was great timing. It took me no time to get it running and drive it away from there. It was a big old petrol engine again – they're fairly simple to troubleshoot.

We were living in the south-east around this time and I got roped into a heist. Some guys on site had spotted some scrap aluminium on an old airfield nearby, and invited me on a mission to go and liberate it. These guys were 'brew crew': they lived to drink. I liked them, liked their nihilistic approach. We set off in their Transit pick-up truck one night and, halfway across the runway, ran out of petrol. It was so out-to-lunch it was like a comedy sketch. Someone ran back to get some, while we sat hoping not to be seen. Then we hooked up an aircraft wing and dragged it off the airfield and up the road to our site – it was madness. We left a huge drag mark in the road all the way to our site – we weren't going to be hard to find. We sliced it up through the night with a petrol saw and hit the road to be at the scrapyard to 'weigh it in' by early morning – job done.

My second son, Sam, was born on the road – not literally. Karen went to the hospital to have him. It was late on Thursday 12 May, and I was like 'if you hang on for a bit it'll be Friday the 13th'. It was half in jest, but that's what happened. I went to pick them both up a day or so later in the fire engine. The nurses were not happy to hand Sam over.

It's a weird feeling having people question your right to be with your kid, but that's what it was. It would be five years before Sam experienced living in a house – it's not done him any harm.

For the next couple of years, most winters we visited a scrapyard just outside Swindon, to either do a bit of work or work on a new vehicle, usually both – and would emerge from there in springtime in something different. I became friends with the guy that owned it, Tony – we're still in touch.

My favourite vehicle was the Bedford RL (4x4) flatbed that I rescued from the gas axe. All that was wrong was the engine. I worked to pay for it, 20 quid a day, and rebuilt the engine in the middle of the field we lived in – and gave it new life.

Then we bought an army surplus mobile workshop, basically a very strong box made to go on the back of an army lorry, for 100 quid. We sat it on the back of this new lorry, strapped it on, and lived in it.

But that meant the lorry couldn't be used for work. I needed a way to take that box on and off the back of the lorry fairly easily – legs on the box would do it. But they would need to be wide enough for me to drive the lorry under the box, in and out, yet no wider than the lorry when on the road.

They needed to be detachable, so I devised a way to connect the legs to the box by sliding a metal beam through them and the box. I could make the legs wide that way, which also helped stability. No bolts – gravity did the work. And the vertical movement of the legs came from using two big tubes, one inside the other; as I jacked the outer section up, lifting the box, a series of holes in each tube would pass each other – and with a large metal pin through these holes I could hold the leg in place, allowing me to remove the jack. I'd raise the legs, one after the other, until it was high enough, drive out, and then lower them in the same way. It was a bit wobbly at full extension, so lowering it made it safer to live in.

It was Thunderbirds meets convoy.

I had a flatbed lorry for the first time and it was 4x4, but for scrapping and other work it really needed a hydraulic crane.

I found one in the yard (and worked to pay it off), took the bed of the lorry off and fitted the crane just behind the cab, shortened the bed and bunged it back on. Now I had a really useful lorry, 4x4, flatbed with a hydraulic arm – it was a 3-tonne crane that could lift just over a tonne at a long reach. It had extendable legs, powered by hydraulics. I wanted legs like that for the box we were living in, but I would need four – two cranes' worth.

It was a fab truck. I spent the next winter in Stroud painting it and getting it ready for its plate (the truck version of an MOT) – and got it, which made this one road legal. That was my first stay in Stroud.

Amusingly around this time I got stopped by a cop, not an unusual event, was harassed a bit and given a 'producer', a ticket that required me to take certain documents to a cop shop within five days. Stuff like an MOT or insurance certificate.

All the time I'd been on the road until now, whenever this happened, I made up a name – never hid that, and threw the ticket away, sometimes screwing it up in front of the cops (if they were rude) because there was nothing they could do. But by this time I was legit.

This time though, the cop was so worked up he forgot to tick any of the boxes – the boxes which specified which documents I had to take in – on this ticket. He'd given me a blank 'producer'. So I took that ticket in and when the cop asked me what documents I was producing I said none, pointing out that all the boxes were blank so I needed to show nothing. I smiled and left. The cop that issued the ticket was so embarrassed. He caught up with me later on the road, fuming. But powerless.

We began to visit Glastonbury at some point in the late eighties; it became a fixture, and in the early days we got in by driving through the perimeter fence somewhere. Someone always made a hole, we were basically squatting, but that evolved over the years. Eventually we had tickets to work there. We made a bit of a transition in these few years, and Glastonbury was at the heart of it. We'd been outlaws, experienced the Beanfield, fled the country, essentially lived on the run, came back and then transitioned into a different version of travelling lifestyle.

My last home on the road was the ex-US Air Force radar trailer, bought from a different yard, for scrap value again. This trailer eventually had a small windmill on the roof. I towed it with the fire engine for a few years. And then I towed it with the flatbed crane lorry when we sold the tow truck – that was a big deal, a big change for me. Sam wasn't keen. We'd driven it to the guy buying it and jumped in a van to leave. Sam was four, something like that, and said, 'What about the truck, Dad?' I told him we'd sold it – it made him sad. Then I passed him the bundle of cash we'd got – that made him grin. It was bittersweet though – that truck had been my home for probably five years and a big part of my life. And his.

I found loads to do at Glastonbury. I used to tow vehicles in, out and around the site – over the mud (which was a hoot) – and picked up a bunch of site-clearance jobs during the festival and at the end. We ended up staying on site for a month or more after the festival ended – it was a great place to live and work. In maybe four festivals I never saw a single band, or wanted to.

I remember the transition from squatter to part of the team. It was my tow truck that opened that door. I bumped into Michael Eavis on site one day. He'd always ask who you were and how long you were planning to stay – he was bold but decent. I was on my way out of the gate to tow someone who'd broken down when we made the connection – broken-down traveller vehicles blocking the approach roads to the festival were a hassle for him and the cops. I offered to tow them for him. He could pay me and we could solve everyone's problems; the festival's, the cops' and the travellers'. And he went for it.

I had a business card handmade by a good friend of mine, Mick, with my mobile phone number – it's how I got jobs. The phone was one of those first-generation ones, hand portable was the euphemistic description – size of two house bricks, lead acid battery-powered, good for one hour's use, not more. I kept mine plugged into my lorry – so no problem.

I gave Michael a card and then I visited the cop control room on site, bold as you like, gave them a card too and told them I was working for the festival and if they had a vehicle that needed moving, just to call me, day or night. I wanted to make sure they knew. And it worked like a charm, they called me all the time. It was a weird thing too, answering the phone to the cops, asking me to go rescue a broken-down traveller. Topsy-turvy that.

Michael opened up a field nearby as he didn't want to be paying to tow uninvited guests on to the festival site, which was understandable.

I had one line I wouldn't cross: I would only tow someone that wanted to be towed. I wouldn't be a tool of the police or of the festival against travellers. This brought me into conflict one night when I got a call to go to the main gate. There was a traveller vehicle half in and half out, refusing to move. Michael was there, it was getting heated – he told me to hitch it up and drag it away. I was pretty sure the driver didn't want that, wasn't broken down, was just trying to get in. I went to speak to him and that's how it was. And so I said I wouldn't do it. It felt like this would break everything. Michael was angry and frustrated; in his view he paid me to tow stuff, I should just do it. But he got his head round it, got over it and we carried on. Just as well. I was unmovable on that.

It was around this time (I was about 30) when my parents told me my grandmother was a Gypsy, a Romany. It explained a lot. Not just how I felt about towns and houses and travelling and stuff, but about the way my aunts were, how they looked and spoke – the fuss they made over me as a kid, always saying how much I looked like their mother. They were different. I felt that. I felt an affinity with them.

I never understood why my mother would say my father 'had a touch of the tar brush in him' – it was Norfolk, racism there is about as casual as it gets, but still. This explained that. It didn't really explain their hostility when Gypsies parked down the road, or maybe it did. And it must have been a mare to deal with – me hitting the road, following my inner Gypsy.

I'd always felt affinity for the Gypsies I met on the road too – maybe this was why. It was in my blood. Amusingly a term used by Gypsies for non-Gypsies is 'gorger' and it's a comment on the overconsumption of people living in houses.

It was a very interesting revelation.

The last few years we went to Glastonbury we did something creative and radical and fun. It was before mobile phones were a thing – they were around but rare. I'd seen BT setting up landline phones down in Babylon (the main site) and selling phone calls at £1 a minute and thought I could do the same. We were based at the top end of the site, a long way from any infrastructure.

Mobile phones would do the job but I needed to charge them and for that I decided to use a windmill. I had an idea, made a sketch of it and showed it to the people organising the Green Field. They liked it and gave us a pitch for the next festival.

I bought an old electricity pylon, it was actually unused, so new but old. I found it sat on the floor of a scrapyard near Hereford – all the best stuff used to come from scrapyards.

It was basically a bunch of metal pieces with holes in – like a Meccano set – designed to be bolted together in a particular way. This one had never been put together, I could see that.

Normally pylons are wider at the base than the top, but I needed something different – so I rearranged it to assemble into four parallel sections which were each 15 feet long and square so that I could stack and carry all four at once on the back of my lorry. I would bolt these four sections together on the ground into a 60-foot single-piece tower, add the windmill to the top and then lift it into the air with my crane.

The problem was the crane I had only went up to about 20 foot and the tower was 60 – I couldn't lift it from the top. Nor could I lift it horizontally from the midpoint and then gently rotate it vertical – that needed 30 foot in height. I had to lift it horizontally from well below the middle (balance point) and, as it rose, apply load to the bottom (short end) to keep the tower horizontal until it was 20 foot in the air and then winch the short side underneath, turning it vertical and lower to the ground.

It wasn't too hard to conceive but was tricky to perform. Once upright, before detaching the crane, I'd bolt on a set of spreaders to widen the base and then drive in some earth anchors from our mast work to hold up this 60-foot free-standing tower.

On top I had a 1kW two-bladed machine from the US (20 times the output of the one on my trailer) and underneath some old train batteries from a scrapyard in Stroud.

I climbed that tower to put up some fairy lights. A guy from the *Observer* took a picture. It was a dodgy experience – I was glad to get back down. It would be a poor way to go.

It was the early days of wind power. I was asked a couple of times about the safety of the windmill – what happened if a blade flew off? I'd say, breezily, that the blades were made of special material that disintegrated on impact, no problem – that did the job. Maybe there's always been a bit of the populist in me.

I hired four transportable phones and set them up at the base of the tower, plugged into the train batteries, and called the whole thing Windphones – it went down a storm.

For the whole of the festival there were queues four wide (one at each phone) and ten or twenty people deep. Everyone said the same thing, 'I'm calling you from a Windphone, whatever that is,' and they would look up at the windmill and say, 'I don't know what happens when the wind stops.' It was mad just how much this caught the imagination, and also how dead useful it was. When I first told people I was going to do it, they said it wouldn't work; who wanted to make a phone call in the middle of a festival? It was ever thus ...

We had requests from people, excited by it, to have one at home and I felt bad puncturing that bubble of excitement, explaining it was just a mobile phone powered by a windmill.

That venture created a lot of cash, in our terms, back then. It was like it rained money; we had bags and bags of change. We used it to buy equipment to help build and install our masts – it was a vital part of that. And great fun.

It was also the source of an interesting legal experience.

For one Glastonbury I booked four phones from a company in Stroud, in the same offices as I worked; come the day to pick them up, they didn't have them. They laughed about it, taunted me – it was deliberate, they didn't try to hide that. They knew Glastonbury was a big thing to us. I think they were actually jealous, being in the mobile business themselves. It was a naff thing to do.

I scrambled about to find alternatives and after the festival went to see them, to tell them what I thought. They called the cops, thinking that calling them was a scary threat to make. People did that all the time on the road. I stayed until they arrived. One spoke to me outside the office, the other spoke to these two guys – and they were brazen or stupid enough to tell that cop that I had booked the phones but they didn't deliver them and there was nothing I could do about it. On his way out that cop told me what they said and that he would give evidence to that effect if I wanted him to (that was pretty impressive) – so I sued them for breach of contract. Breach of verbal contract.

Lawyers will tell you a verbal contract is a contract, it's binding in the same way as a written one – it's just harder to prove. These guys thought it was their word against mine – and it was until they told the cops. I put that wrong right and it felt good.

I was living on a hill outside Stroud by this time. It was our base, where we left all this festival hardware, tower sections, train batteries (they were not small) – and from where we made and installed our wind-monitoring masts.

My time on the road was a great experience. It was an adventure. I got to do some imaginative things, problem-solving, building stuff, I travelled, partied – and it either taught me or helped me to hone my resilience, self-reliance and boldness.

Nothing fazed me, which is why I happily took that leap into the unknown and dropped back in to try and build a really big windmill on that hill.

Travelling equipped me perfectly for that, mentally and physically – and literally. I had the tools to make that first mast and that was the key to the whole thing.

CHAPTER 5
EPIPHANY

I don't know how many epiphanies I've had in my life – it will have been a few – but none as clear and as life-changing as this one. Or as exciting.

Although, ten years earlier, deciding to leave town and live on the road had those same attributes and the same feeling. It was a radical, exciting leap into the unknown – in both cases.

It was the winter of 1991. I was parked on a hill near Stroud, about a decade into this life – on the road and off the grid – using small windmill to power my life.

Britain's first big windmills (the modern versions) were built in November that year at Delabole in Cornwall. I went to see them for myself, I had to.

The idea of really big windmills was fascinating and exciting at the same time.

A few months before that, parked on a different hill and looking at the town below, I tried to imagine how much power was being used, just to light the night – and thought it daunting.

The little windmill on the roof of my trailer made 50 watts when the wind was blowing hard. It charged the old train batteries I'd rescued from a scrapyard, and ran a couple of low-voltage lights and a water pump. Not much. Soon I would also be using it to run a laptop as I started to crunch wind data, but more on that in a bit.

The amount of energy being used in the town below me was so much more than I was able to make – it didn't look feasible that wind energy as I knew it could replace fossil fuels. At the same time I was aware of climate change and that the way electricity was made in Britain was the biggest single cause of it. I felt that had to change. Renewable energy, rooted in alternative culture and small-scale, needed to become mainstream. Delabole was an indication that that might be possible.

It was this combination of thoughts that led to the epiphany I had on the top of that hill – and it was simple: I could spend another ten years living a low-impact life myself, or I could drop back in and try to build a big windmill on this hill. And have a bigger impact that way.

It was a simple but radical thought. A precursor to big change.

I knew the hill I lived on was windy, I knew how small windmills worked. I had a lifelong concern for sustainability. I'd taken low-impact living as far as I arguably could. It was a pretty logical decision in that respect. I had no idea what this would take, or how long, but it seemed to me that it must be possible.

The challenge invigorated me – at times in the next few years I felt like I was using my brain for the first time. Building a big windmill, as I discovered, was a blend of scientific, technical and commercial propositions, of aerodynamics, mechanics, electronics, statistics . . . I had mountains to learn.

Wind data, for example, was a deep and complex subject. The measurement of the wind resource on a site was vital. The data itself was relatively simple to capture, but data quality was paramount; the cube law relationship between windspeed and energy in the wind means that small measuring errors translate into large prediction errors. Collecting data on site was one thing, but the process of producing a 20-year forecast from that was something else. I learned that local topography has a bearing on windspeed and turbulence (which reduces power), the shape of the land several kilometres away mattered (who knew?) and even the 'roughness' of the surface itself (grass being ideal, trees much less so).

Wind data and its use was a fascinating subject, a developing field of knowledge, vital to early wind-energy projects and ultimately the development of the wind industry that would follow.

There was more to come, each a deep topic – windmill technology, planning and environment assessments, grid compatibility, financial modelling, construction.

I took a logical approach. Every topic, every field of science, of engineering (of human endeavour) has a language and a set of rules. They might be the laws of physics or the laws of man – it doesn't matter, everything can be understood this way. I learned the language and rules of each and applied them to this project. And I had fun, such fun doing this – it absorbed me completely.

I think it was the perfect challenge at the perfect time. It suited my circumstances and my nature. And my interests.

I'm averse to doing things other people think I should or tell me to. I look at and do things my own way – it's got me into plenty of trouble, but it's also a bit of a superpower.

The tougher things get, the harder I try – it spurs me on. The harder anyone pushes me, the harder I push back – it's like a law of physics.

I'm stubborn, I know that. I don't quit, I don't let anything go – detail matters to me but the big picture matters too. You have to see both and know when to focus on one and when to focus on the other. I struggle to take no for an answer, especially if there's no good reason coming with it. I'm irrepressible when something matters to me. Obsessive? Yeah, that's fair.

These facets of my character lent themselves to this challenge – in this way I was qualified, if not in any other. I think my life on the road helped too.

I've learned the importance of looking for another way to do things – not for the sake of it but because there's so much potential if you arrive at a problem fresh, without baggage or dogma. I see no merit in doing things the way they've always been done just because that's how they've always been done.

When judging what might be possible you need to balance competing factors. You need to be mindful of what's possible today, while at the same time being relatively agnostic to that – looking past what's possible to what might become possible. Things change, sometimes a different approach is enough. It's a mistake to judge an idea only by what's possible today or what already has been done.

In wind energy in those early years I found dogma and misjudgement, in the choice of technology and in the likelihood I could pull this off.

Henry Ford's famous quote springs to mind – before he got started making cars he said if he'd asked his customers what they wanted, they would have said faster horses.

Sometimes you need a new paradigm, not the stretching of an old one.

As I was to learn, nobody would think I could do this – drop back in and build a big windmill on this hill with no money, no qualifications and no experience. Windmills had the aura of a crazy idea anyway and so that was understandable on the face of it – an easy mistake to make. Being underestimated was part of it, that was something I was used to; it's often an advantage.

I took the challenge one piece at a time and the things that didn't look possible at the outset became so later. Maybe I was lucky, maybe I made my own luck – probably it was a bit of both. I certainly persisted.

So there I was, ten years of living on the road behind me, in need of a new challenge. And this came along.

I wasn't contemplating running a business or going any further than building one big windmill on the hill I was living on – but that itself was enough. A big enough ambition.

Lots of people have ideas but don't pursue them. It's easy to be trapped in a comfort zone, to not want to take risks. Even people who made the jump to go travelling, a big lifestyle change, for some it became a place to stay, a familiar lifestyle, maybe itself a comfort zone, an ideological parking place.

Money traps people too, of course. I saw friends, travellers and others, who became dependent on the dole. When you have next to nothing, breaking away from something, however small, is a challenge. However restricting it feels to be there, the uncertainty of not being there, of not having that small something, is a barrier.

On the road I saw people become attached to a particular signing-on office and therefore a particular site and, in that way, chained to a place and the 20 quid a week or so that it was back then. It was barely anything but it was more than nothing. It was a trap – not an intentional one, but one of dependency. A bare minimum status quo to cling on to, like a lifebelt. I'd felt that in towns and seen it on the road. I wanted to be free of that.

I experienced it also in the scrapyard where I worked from time to time. I could get paid 20 quid a day, doesn't sound like much but it was relative to others there – as I had skills, breaking down engines and cutting up vehicles, that was actually fun in small doses, with the 'gas axe'.

But 20 quid a day was a limiting thing too – not just the money itself but the cost of a day of my life. A day when I couldn't do anything else. I had a breakdown truck, I worked with it when I could – breakdowns and scrapping mostly – if I got one job I could earn a week's scrapyard pay and spend time working on my truck (it always needed something). Or I could do something else. But to get that job I had to stop working and go looking. Take the risk of finding nothing or take the money – and be unable to look and unable to do anything else.

I've often struggled with the concept of committing to something, that sounds odd I reckon, coming from me, but

My first bike, a Garelli, taken in 1976.

My favourite bike, the one I rode at the Battle of the Beanfield, a Ducati 450.
This picture was taken back in the 80s but I still have this bike.

My friend Mike, my son Dane and a helpful copper (left to right) at the Molesworth eviction – this was in the *Guardian* in 1984.

Pulling a broken down truck on to Graffham Water, just after Molesworth, with my breakdown truck in a winter during the mid-80's.

The fire engine tow truck that I took to Europe.

Me, Brian and Tim (left to right) load testing a ground anchor on a mast site in 1992.

Me climbing the windphone tower at Glastonbury, 1994.

My 4x4 Bedford with a crane on the back, fire engine in the background, at Glastonbury in the early 90s.

My 4x4 Bedford at the scrap yard where I worked sometimes - the army box behind it had just had its legs fitted. That's a brake cylinder sitting on the roof, waiting to be fitted.

Tim and another guy load testing a ground anchor in Scotland in the early 90s. We had a white out and got stuck way back down the hill. This is us winching our way out of some more bad ground.

when you are doing something you exclude the possibility of doing anything else – and that has bothered me most of my life, kept me drifting at times, in neutral, not engaged in something, so that I was free to do anything. Sometimes that's a thought process in a day, about choices made in a day – sometimes it's lasted much longer.

I did a bit of both at the scrapyard, mixing certainty with adventure. Working there helped the guy that owned it too and sometimes I did it for trucks or truck parts instead of cash – but the tension between the two was clear to me a couple of times. I saw people that were still there every time I visited over many years. That suits plenty of people of course, routine and some certainty. I'm not knocking it. Just saying that it can also hold you back. You don't know what's out there if you don't go looking.

People can hold you back too. The world is tribal, made up of groups of people who self-identify to one degree or another and see others as outsiders. I've been an outsider for much of my life, since being a kid; I've made the transition to the inside of various groups and eventually needed to leave because it was restricting. People don't want other people to change, they think they know you and they resist change – in the same way they resist change more generally.

The world of travelling wasn't immune from this. It could be cliquey – it had a look, a dress code if you like, much born of practicality but also choice.

Travelling had its own code (there was more than one version though – travellers weren't overly homogeneous in that respect). I could see the restrictions imposed by collective identity, travelling, as I had in other walks of life. But it was still freer than anywhere I'd been before.

Inverted snobbery is a common denominator among people, among tribes, though all snobbery comes from a place of perceived superiority, like racism – so I think to call it 'inverted snobbery' is rather imperfect as it assumes by definition that there is an actual merit order, which gets reversed. When in fact it's all in the mind of the beholder. It was interesting to see that – even in a very radical culture. People are people though, and it's been my experience, at school, as a biker and a traveller and in the word of business. Oh and in football, very much so. The snobs in football talk about 'football people': it identifies the insiders.

It's about identity, belonging and being seen to belong. I get that and I've felt that and appreciated it in different tribes. There's a good feeling within that mutual affirmation: relative safety being part of a herd and not standing out (dress code especially speaks to this). But, of course, the flip side is the restriction.

I've lived with little and with no money. One night in a layby, on the way to the Stones, I had some change in my pocket. I remember picking it out and throwing it over the hedge. And then I had nothing. I liked that feeling. I tried to live that way for a while. I got hungry. Not for the first time.

Over time I learned that some money is essential. How you get it and what you do with it is key.

What's important is not to chase money, not to let that be your purpose in life. This choice is best illustrated by asking this question, do you live to eat or eat to live? I eat to live.

Money is a tool, like a spanner, but a bit more universal – maybe an adjustable spanner …

Living on the road was a great experience. I learned about myself and about people and the way of the world – well, some of the ways. It made me resourceful and more self-reliant. I was my own electrician, plumber and mechanic … though less good at woodwork. I marvelled at how in more normal life people worked all day to pay other people to do these things for them.

I took that into business, that self-sufficient outlook, being end-to-end with a minimum of middlemen, it made great sense at the start, of course, having very little money – but 'in-housing' everything we could became a principle by which Ecotricity lived. And not just for economic reasons; I believe if something is important then you should do it yourself (if you can). Take responsibility for it, understand the topic completely and be more in control that way, of quality not least – but timing also. It's like being able to fix your own engines. When you can do that, the benefits are not just practical and immediately obvious, they endure and it's a spiritual thing, the way it makes you feel – not understanding how stuff works is frustrating and isolating.

Globalisation has always seemed illogical to me. How does it make sense to 'offshore' jobs to other countries, to outsource industries and manufacturing to the far sides of the world? Because it was cheaper in the short term. For a while it was all the rage in Britain – but we made ourselves dependent and created holes in our own economy doing this.

Privatisation of large chunks of the public sector, which began in the mid nineties, is another great example of a dogma which has never lived up to its promise, never delivered better or cheaper services to the public, to the nation. It was arguably 'another way' to do things, but driven by ideology not logic, and doomed to fail unless it just got lucky …

Sometimes you can be right for the wrong reasons. Privatisation was just wrong.

In energy, it was laid bare. Public energy companies were sold on the cheap; the sale price in billions looked like a win but of course the gain was a one-off, and the idea that ordinary people could own shares and make money this way was a chimera. The City made a lot of money as post-flotation share prices rose for only one reason: the assets were undervalued. Then, to reduce costs and increase profitability for shareholders, tens of thousands of people were made redundant and that cost fell to the state; it cost society, just as it benefitted the new private owners. The efficiencies that privatisation was meant to deliver came from mass redundancies. Not some kind of business rocket science. Nothing was gained on the flip side. And the industry simply went from being a public monopoly serving the public to being a private one serving its shareholders. It is now mostly foreign owned.

The energy industry is a regulated oligopoly now. The 'free market', that oxymoron-in-chief, was never so obviously absent as in energy. And private ownership has shown itself to be incapable of the long-term view and investment which vital infrastructure like this needs (kinda why it was built with public money originally) and incompatible with our national interest.

Living on the road also brought me closer to the natural world. The real bare necessities of living and the natural cycles of day and night – and the seasons. Of course, the seasons are fundamentally different; living on the road you feel the impacts so much more.

My first winter living without a house highlighted this to me. Because there were no lights, when night fell everything stopped. If you'd not sorted yourself out by then you were stuck until morning. And it was easy to be stuck until spring if you parked in the wrong place. In that first winter camp in Wales where I swapped my ambulance for a bus, the bus had been driven downhill through the woods and parked nose first. Winter came and it was stuck. That's how I got such a great swap. I learned a lot about off-road driving while living on the road, most of my later vehicles were four-wheel drive – this was my first off-road experience with a bus. The way out was uphill, in the mud, and travelling backwards. This bus had no chance. Lots of people had tried.

When the time came to leave, I went and knocked on the door of a farmer across the road from our woods. He was also a local councillor and someone that really didn't like us being there, we knew that – he was hostile. But he had a big four-wheel drive tractor – an off-road beast. It was a Sunday and when he came to the door he was about to have lunch. I just said that I wanted to leave the woods, I knew he wanted that too – and my vehicle was stuck. If he would come and give me a tow, I'd be on my way. It was cheeky but had a logic to it. He agreed to do it and came down after lunch. It was a wild ride. We hooked up a tow rope to the back of the bus and I jumped in the front, engine running, and off he went, aggressively. He got traction and just kept going, it felt very fast – going backwards, up the twisty muddy gap in between the trees, with little in the way of steering. But we made it without too much damage – usually bodywork is what went first on buses, just added to the image, like a scar – and I pulled along the road and parked on the verge to get ready to leave to go to Molesworth.

It was a good experience that; my enemy became my friend for that brief moment and we both got what we wanted.

Winters were more longer, damper and colder living this way; spring and summer a relative joy. We would emerge like creatures from hibernation, ready to party.

Living on the road connected me more to living itself. I converted trailers, trucks and buses to live in, found ways to work with trucks I built – and eventually made my own power using small windmills.

That gave me an understanding of renewable energy and energy itself. How hard it is to make it, how valuable it is. The difference it makes to life. Windmills connected me to the environment in another way. I was always conscious, wherever I parked, if it was a windy spot or not because it made a difference that I could see.

In a house, you turn on taps and flick switches and don't think much about it, perhaps until you see the bill. Where it comes from and how it's made what impact it has: we lack appreciation of these things. It's not just water and power.

Food is a great example. We're detached from the cruelty and suffering of animal farming by shrink-wrapped, sanitised products and misdirection through marketing. We eat 'products' and we have little idea where they come from or how they are made.

This detachment extends across life as we know it and is a key driver of unsustainability and the climate crisis.

Modern living takes much from us.

CHAPTER 6
MISSION IMPOSSIBLE?

I had no idea how big the challenge was. This was pre internet, there was no Google, no Siri to ask. I didn't even know what I needed to know. Years later, Donald Rumsfeld would talk of known unknowns and unknown unknowns (in the deceitful build-up to the Gulf War); this is where we were: there was no manual for this. I knew some of what I needed to know and guessed there was more.

But there was somewhere I could go.

Cornwall, to the site of Britain's first wind farm.

I drove down and knocked on the door of the farmhouse. I wanted to see those windmills mostly, but also, if I could, I wanted to say hello and see what I could learn. Peter Edwards answered the door and he was happy to chat – I got a lot from that, not detail or numbers but a steer and a feeling.

The one big thing I learned that day in Cornwall was that these machines were fixed speed – they ran at the same speed whatever the weather. That was a surprise. I thought I'd seen them speed up and down with the wind, which is intuitive, but Peter put me right on that and it seems it was a common misconception. These windmills ran at one speed however strong the wind. That may not sound important – but turned out to be a crucial decision point for me months later when looking to choose the right wind technology.

I went back to Stroud encouraged by what I'd seen and by my conversation with Peter. And a bit excited.

My ambition was just to build a big windmill on the hill that I was living on, no more than that. I had no idea how big a job that actually was, but I knew the hill I was on was windy – everything else I would discover and learn.

I dived in, head first. It was all brand new, not just to me but to itself. Wind energy was an emerging field, dominated at the time by academia, that's where it grew from a world of research, theory and R&D – research and development. There was a lot to know, and I had to start by finding out what I needed to know. Who could not be excited by that?

It took five years to build that first windmill, and by the time it was finished I'd been through the whole wind-development process – undertaken every step, learning each of them by doing. That became the blueprint for what followed: the next windmills and ultimately the generation arm of Ecotricity – a company called Next Generation. I'm a bit of a *Star Trek* fan and the name seemed more than right for the job in hand, building the next forms of energy generation – the green ones.

I started by reading whatever I could find (*Windpower Monthly* was pretty much it), attending events held by the fairly new British Wind Energy Association, speaking with people in this emerging industry, mostly academics and enthusiasts, and I pieced together the puzzle this way.

The first thing I discovered was the need to measure the wind at the height of the machine I intended to build – back then it was 30 metres. This data was fundamental to a business plan, to the economic model showing that a project was financially sustainable. I needed that to persuade a bank to lend me the money to build it, but funding was a problem for later.

I needed a 30-metre mast. I didn't have the money to buy one but I reckoned I could make one – I'd seen one in Wales, it was basically metal tubes with flanges welded on each end, a bunch of guy wires holding it up and some ground anchors. Not rocket science. So I made one and used my Bedford 4x4 with the crane on the back to put it up, on top of the hill I was living on. It was a bit hairy at times but it went up and stayed up. Which was a bonus.

With that step accomplished, while we spent the next year collecting data, I turned to the next parts of the puzzle: getting planning consent, a grid connection to export the power and finding the money to build it. But before that I had to decide on technology – what kind of windmill to build there.

I found a two-day course at Imperial College London. I was probably unique in the audience as someone who wanted to build a project rather than being a student per se. And it showed in my interrogation of some of the industry players who were giving lectures – and not being very forthcoming with their numbers … It seemed only I thought that the cost of a foundation was a vital piece of information.

It was on this course that I started to explore the key technology choice that needed to be made – windmills up until then were of the fixed speed type. The electricity they made was synchronised to the grid with a gearbox – the windspeed could rise or fall but the speed of revolution of the blades stayed the same. This had inherent drawbacks.

I'd already learned of the cube law relationship between windspeed and energy in the wind – basically, if you double the windspeed the energy in it increases eightfold. This fact underpins much in modern wind engineering and in site selection. For a fixed speed windmill, it means that gusts of wind cause massive power spikes to be absorbed mechanically in the gearbox and drivetrain.

I'd heard of another approach: variable speed windmills which synchronised to the grid electronically, speeding up and down with the gusts and not just avoiding mechanical stress this way, but using that energy in the wind to make electricity instead. They had other advantages – being gearless made them much quieter and the noise they did make was all aerodynamic, not mechanical. That sounded good to me. More intuitive.

I raised this with the lecturers on this crash course at Imperial and the consensus was that it was a good idea in theory but variable speed machines were too expensive to make and fixed speed was the way to go. I was unconvinced. And that led me to go knock on another door.

But before I did that I spoke to Brian, the guy who owned the hill I was living on. I told him what I thought was possible. He liked it and said let's do it.

We'd become friends in the few months I'd been living on his land. He was a free spirit in every sense, living for the moment, unfazed by what people thought of him or what might be expected – a rebel living on his own land without planning permission. He lived in a totally dilapidated old caravan – it's not possible to describe how broken down and filthy it was. He was off-grid, but didn't even have any lights. He had a tiny black-and-white TV, which he sat in front of each night, run from a car battery. And that was it.

One of the first things I did when we moved on to his land was to hook up a windmill on a telegraph pole by his trailer and set up some lights for him. He'd seen ours and was interested – it changed his life. And got him interested in wind energy.

He was up for the challenge. We formed a partnership, called it Western Windpower and set about it.

Nobody else believed we could do this – just me, him and Karen, my partner from travelling days and mother of my second son, Sam.

This was especially true of Brian's family. I was pretty unpopular with them, they saw this as a con. Brian was in his seventies, if I was a woman there's no doubt I would have been a gold digger in their eyes. They were worried about his land, which they expected to inherit. They thought I wanted it. I didn't. He offered it to me before he died and I refused it. And I promised him I would pay his share from the project to his family for as long as the windmill was up there – and I've kept that promise.

He never saw it built, but he never doubted it would be. I recall our last conversation. It was to say goodbye and he told me then he knew I would build it.

That first step, measuring the wind resource on site, wasn't just the essential first step of any wind project: the way we did that was fundamental to making this project happen. I made my own tower because I didn't have the money to buy one, but I did have the tools to make one. I had cutting and welding equipment and a crane, and a totally can-do attitude.

And it turned into a business, making masts for other people – which in turn paid for the next steps I needed to take.

At first we made our masts in the open air on the hill we were living on, dodging the weather. We'd drive them somewhere remote and spend days in the middle of nowhere putting them up, drive home and make another one. It was a cottage-industry-style thing, intense and fun and productive. Later, we bought a yard and got more professional – our range went from the original 30 metres all the way up to 100 metres as windmills kept getting taller. And we brought some intuition to the design. By then we were making slot-together masts, shorter sections, lighter and quicker to assemble than flanged – but also we made them tapering. They didn't need to be the same size at the bottom as at the top like everybody else's were. And we exported our masts all over the world – to the US, Australia, Japan, Europe, all sorts of places. It was fun.

Solving that first step by making our own mast was a little piece of magic, I had little or no money and no idea what it would cost to do the other steps. I was taking these issues one at a time, as they presented, but at the same time aware they were coming. If I'd looked at the whole problem, the logical answer would have been that it wasn't possible – but by chipping away I had a chance. The mast business enabled everything that followed, all of the chipping away.

I was entering this with no experience, no qualifications, no money. The odds were stacked, the mission looked impossible. I like it that way.

Building that first windmill took five years. It started with wind monitoring; technology choice for the windmill itself came next – that led me to knock on the door of a small wind company in Germany, called Enercon. They had a variable speed machine with a gearbox at that time, a kind of hybrid, but emerging technology that was variable speed with no gearbox – for me that was the holy grail. My small windmills had all been like this, it made the most sense. I gleaned this from magazine snippets (thank you, *Windpower Monthly*).

I couldn't get a response from Enercon by fax so I spent my last few hundred quid on some clothes and a plane ticket and went to see them. That was the start of another fantastic part of the journey and decades-long relationship.

The technology chosen and two hybrid machines identified as the best fit for the site, the next step was planning and environmental assessments like wildlife, noise and visual impact.

Visual impact was a key issue. We needed a photomontage to show how windmills would look in the landscape – that was a challenge, this was pre Photoshop (almost pre PC). We ended up with a technique that was more photocollage than anything. I worked with a local photographer called John, a friend of a friend; he took shots of our hill from different local vantage points, projected them on to a wall in his studio and placed cardboard cut-out windmills into the projection, zooming in or out to achieve an approximation of the right scale – and then re-photographed the whole thing. It was ingenious (his idea not mine) and it worked really well.

Incredibly we got planning permission at the first time of asking. I recall an angry councillor at that meeting, spluttering that 'this was ridiculous', that I didn't have 'two pennies to rub together' and he wasn't wrong. I was a guy living in a trailer on a hill – a lot of people found that challenging. At the same time, in a letter to our local paper, somebody else talked about mighty oaks growing from little acorns – he was also correct, metaphorically and later literally, as we grew to become the biggest employer in Stroud over the next decade or two.

So we had planning permission for two 30-metre-high hybrid machines, but by then the technology had moved on and we needed to build one 40-metre machine of the new gearless version. A super-exciting prospect to me. And an easy ask of the planners, I thought, but a group called the Country Guardians had started up in the meantime and they were spreading virulent anti-wind propaganda. They targeted us, we were refused planning permission and had to appeal.

That was another learning curve: the appeals process – which we won in the end.

Job done, we thought, but the National Trust had other ideas; they started proceedings in the High Court to challenge the legality of our planning permission. It was another interesting episode, a test of our resolve and ability to fund a defence, their case had no merit – eventually they pulled out and paid our costs. But because I represented myself that amounted to almost nothing. Rather than cash it I put the cheque on the wall of our office (we had one by then). It was a sweet victory.

The other challenge we had to overcome was a grid connection for exporting our electricity. Since the first planning permission, I'd been having a running battle with the local grid company.

I contacted them right at the start of the project, because I knew you needed an affordable grid connection as much as you needed good wind to make a project work. They told me to come back when I had planning permission because they 'didn't take the project seriously'. That was a bit shocking I thought, but I went off and got permission; it took a couple of years and when I went back they basically said 'it's a terrible place to put a windmill' and quoted me £1.5 million to connect to the local grid. The whole project was likely to cost a fifth of that so it was a killer – if I accepted it. I didn't. And over the next year or so the quote dropped first to £1 million, then £500,000 (still unaffordable), and eventually we paid something like £36,000 …

That's how hard it used to be to get sense from local grid companies. It was a show stopping event if we'd accepted what they said. Not taking no for an answer is something of a trait of mine, and at times a useful one.

These were the biggest obstacles: wind, planning and grid. With them solved it left only money – how to fund that first project. We could see by then that the total cost of building it was about £350,000. A lot of cash.

Around this time I met Triodos; they were a new kind of bank, an ethical one – something that's still rare today. They were from Holland, just setting up in Britain, and they were willing to not only lend me the money to build the windmill, but to let me build it myself. That's almost unheard of now in a mature industry, but back then it was special. I had no track record, this being my first windmill. The machine we wanted to build had no track record either. Hooking up with Triodos meant we could build this first windmill but also complete the final part of the job ourselves. It was important as it enabled us to travel end-to-end in wind development, from site selection to construction. We created our own blueprint this way of total 'in-housing'. Doing everything ourselves gave us an advantage that enabled us to do things differently.

We still work with Triodos and Enercon nearly 25 years later, and the local guy that did the civil engineering work on that first windmill, Bob, still does all of our civil engineering. Long-term relationships like these are empowering and they only come about through fairness and honesty on both sides. There's nothing much better than working with people you can trust.

Triodos were only willing to fund 80 per cent of the whole project cost though – which meant I needed to find about £60,000. By this time Western Windpower had made that kind of money.

So, the final problem was solved. And I got on with the construction planning, access roads, cranes – and building the foundation, which I now knew the cost of, some of the *really* fun stuff.

But we hit another snag, just as all of these last details fell into place.

It came as the local grid company (the MEB) tried to lay the cable to connect our windmill to the local grid.

They needed to go across a churchyard in the village down the road and our local objectors – we had a few – staged an occupation and sat in the way. It was unexpected and a bit of a threat – no grid connection meant our project was dead – and it got fraught. I pushed the MEB to exercise their statutory powers, to force the issue, and reluctantly they did – only a last-minute call from the Catholic church to Stroud's police chief saying that the protestors had consent to remain in the churchyard prevented a mass arrest of them. Which I would have been OK with – hey, I'd been on that side of things myself.

The issue was eventually resolved, but not without lingering controversy. Somebody raided the churchyard encampment overnight (our objectors were part-timers), and bust it up a bit. I was accused of being behind it but to this day I have no idea who it was. The windmill split local opinion, we'd heard it was local supporters. More controversially, it was claimed the local priest had signed the document to allow the cable through the churchyard without knowing what it was – allegedly he was blind and someone on his staff did this knowingly. I don't know the truth of this, I just know that the occupation ended without arrests and our windmill got connected to the local grid. And we carried on getting ready for the big day when the windmill would arrive.

Getting that big windmill up the narrow lane to the site was the last real hurdle; it was touch and go at times. I remember a friend of mine walking ahead of the low loader with a chainsaw to trim the way through.

We built it on Friday the 13th of December 1996; I'm not superstitious, more like anti-superstitious – I cross roads to walk under ladders, not avoid them. This was a special day, my son Sam was born on a different Friday the 13th. I liked that day.

A lot had happened in five years. I was living in a house. That was not an easy transition. I was running several companies. And my thoughts had already turned to building the next windmill.

We'd overcome so many challenges, grown in a process that today you'd call bootstrapping, and become leading players in this brand new industry. We'd built that first windmill and this was a fundamental moment – so much else would come from this.

I knew that it had been make or break.

My good friend Brian didn't see it, but he knew it would happen.

CHAPTER 7
NECESSITY AND HAPPENSTANCE

I lost an argument to an ant once.

I was in the Rif Mountains of Morocco, with my new haircut, sat on a rock in the sun. It was growing territory and I was stoned – which makes me more sensitive. A line of ants appeared, climbing up over the rock I was sat on, and coming straight at me. I shooed them away, using my fingers as a roadblock. It wasn't so hard. They went slightly into disarray, not sure where to go if they couldn't go the way they wanted. Some short time later, seconds probably, this really big ant comes along. It was a soldier ant, I reckon, and I tried the same thing with my finger – he wasn't put off. He kept coming and while I wasn't keen on making contact, he had no qualms – he won that game of chicken. So I picked up a tiny twig – might have been a leaf stalk – held it between my thumb and one finger and put it between us, like a challenge and a roadblock. Incredibly, he grabbed the stick and pulled it clean out of my fingers and sat there holding it. It was a freaky experience. I was impressed by this ant. I got up and moved.

I started four companies in the first half of the nineties – I never had a plan to, they just happened, for a variety of reasons.

Our first business was born of necessity – I needed a mast to gather wind data, didn't have the money to buy one, so I made one. That's how it started. We learned a lot from that and had a lot of fun.

A farmer in Swindon saw our masts and asked if he could buy one.

Garrad Hassan, a consultancy from Bristol, were next and they needed several. That helped us – the experience and the kudos. To be good enough for them was to be good enough for almost anyone else.

We did some for Wind Prospect too, a small wind development company, like us. We went to Liverpool, Cumbria and the isle of Islay for these guys. Three very different sites, learning all the time.

But Scottish Power were the people that really propelled this new business.

All their sites were remote, some were just more remote than others.

Some we could reach in our truck, some needed the local farm tractor, others a quad bike – some we just had to walk to. The weather and sites were extreme, dramatic and beautiful. I'm a fan of weather, the more extreme the better. The breaks we had, huddled behind a hillock or in our truck if it was there, were treasured, vital. And then it was back into the elements. Windmills need to be built in windy places, of course, there are none as windy as hills in Scotland.

We'd spend the first day or two getting our kit on site and driving in our homemade earth anchors – we attached the guy wires to these and they held the mast up. We made our own test rig for these anchors, using an HGV bottle jack to pull on them while measuring the force applied in tonnes. We needed anchors at four compass points and sometimes we'd get three in and the last would be impossible – ground conditions were probably our biggest challenge – and we'd have to find another location nearby and start all over again. We were driving these in with a sledgehammer, all day – it was long and laborious. We'd take turns until our arms needed a rest.

I like to do things with both hands and so could swap from left to right to left again as each arm tired the other was recovered – only one does real work at a time. That helped a lot. I'd begun using both hands years before; I ate too fast, so fast I got stomach cramps, so I started using chopsticks to slow myself down. But got too fast with those so switched to chopsticks left-handed, that slowed me down for a while. I also chopped wood with both hands; it's a good discipline, to teach yourself to do something with each hand. It involves both sides of the brain, a bit of crossing over, and makes you understand better what you're actually doing. You need to be careful of your fingers at the start, with an axe – not so much the chopsticks.

It was in Scotland one time, we met a group of body-builders, nice guys, curious about what we were doing.

They looked at our sledgehammer and joked about it – they thought it small. Of course it was compared to the weights they trained with: we used a 10-pound sledge, that's about 5 kilograms – like nothing to a body builder. We invited them to give it a go and they came up to site the next day – we half hoped we'd found some help, some muscle, to get this part of the job done. It was hilarious and illuminating to us and them – they could handle this sledgehammer easily, pick it up like it was a toffee hammer, but after about ten swings they were done. They had strength but not stamina – they couldn't swing this for an hour, let alone all day. They were buff, we were wiry – neither of us could do what the other did. Training at three to five repetitions you can lift great weights, put on big muscles, but it's a very limited kind of strength. Working all day with a 10-pound sledge was a different thing. This was a real-world demonstration of the difference. And yeah, it made us feel good …

Once we had four anchors in and tested, we'd spend about a day laying out the mast, the guy wires, attaching the data-logging equipment and sensors, testing that – and sometimes we could get the mast up the same day, often it was the next. It was several days of tough work, in remote locations, wild conditions – topped and tailed with long drives punctuated with café pitstops.

Back in Stroud I'd weld a new mast and drive to Hereford in my old lorry to get it hot-dip galvanised – it's quite something seeing bundles of 4-metre-long tubes get dunked into giant vats of liquid metal. I'd wait and bring it back the same day and get back to packaging everything up for the next trip. There were lots of parts, not least nuts and bolts and clamps.

The last thing you wanted was to be in Scotland on top of a hill and be missing a part. We learned that the hard way.

All of this was outdoors work; we had nowhere to work but the field we lived in and it always seemed to be in the winter. It was a sod's law of wind energy – people only wanted masts in the winter.

We'd install our masts as a team of two or three. It was usually me and Tim – a guy living on Brian's hill when I got there – and whoever else we could get interested. Not many did more than one trip – except me and Tim. We'd spend a few days putting a mast up in the middle of nowhere, each site an adventure, and drive home. I loved it. And it powered our venture.

One time we took our truck to the top of a hill, it was a long off-road trek but not too difficult. We'd been busy all day while it snowed, not realising what it would mean later. When it came time to leave it was a whiteout. We couldn't see any ground details, couldn't see our tracks or the places to avoid – we had to winch ourselves downhill most of the way out of one bog or another as dusk fell. It's rare to struggle to drive downhill off-road when gravity is your friend. But we had no idea what we were driving on, or which way to go other than simply downwards. It was the kind of weather and situation that was potentially life-threatening.

In Stroud we had a small room in a business centre. Our first office. I'd word-process an invoice from there, write a couple more quotes, make some calls – that kind of thing. It was a strange environment for me but we needed an office for practical reasons. I didn't have the proper rent at the start, they wanted about £100 a week. I was honest with the lady running it and said I could pay £50 a week and as soon as someone with all the money came along I'd leave – which kinda worked for everyone. She went for it, that got us started and over the next couple of years we became a good customer, moving several times in that business centre into bigger rooms until we occupied the entire top floor, paying proper rent by then, of course.

Our mast business grew; we gained more customers the more jobs we did. Word-of-mouth was important in this small, emerging industry, as well as reputation. We had some failures and some masts were sabotaged. We adapted our designs for the more serious weather in Scotland, and made them taller as windmills were getting taller. By the time we finished, many years later, we were at 100 metres, an incredible height for tubes of 200 millimetres or so to stand at.

We bought a yard of our own a few years in, became a team of people; got our first website; evolved our masts to be short sections that slotted together (shorter, lighter, quicker to assemble – good for export). We built a machine to make these slot-together tubes ourselves and started exporting them all over the world. We became one of two main mast companies supplying this industry globally – the other was based in the US.

We did everything ourselves, learning as we went, and that became our approach. I took every step of every process from the first time we did something. That wasn't just an economic imperative – it brought longer term benefits from the understanding gained. We'd take those learnings and keep each new thing in-house, creating an ability to do something else. Creating self-reliance. A benefit in itself.

The mast business funded the building of our first windmill, not just the 20 per cent we needed to top up the bank loan, but before we got that far it paid for every other step we had to take, planning, grid and so on. Making masts paid the rent and because we were working in the wind industry we stayed close to the action – learning in the process.

We built this mast business while taking the next steps to develop our own first windmill; they happened alongside each other in those first five years.

The second business I started was, I would say, more out of happenstance.

I was excited by the variable speed concept for big windmills, attracted to it. I'd discovered the small company in Germany that made them but not been able to get much response by fax so I went and knocked on their door – just as I did with the farmer in Wales (to help me evict myself) and just as I did with the farmer in Cornwall (where those first big mills were built) – because really it seemed the only thing I could do.

We got on like a house on fire and the timing was good – Enercon were just exploring export as a next step and during that first visit they asked if I'd like to open a UK office for them. I've a free-ranging imagination – but this was way more than I'd dreamt of, as I flew over Germany imagining what it might have been like in the Second World War, on my way to knock on their door.

I got home excited and super-keen to push on. I needed a better office and somewhere to live – my trailer wasn't going to cut it for much longer. Living on the hill was difficult, we were surrounded by mud – it's how sites are in winter. Brian kept cows, that made it worse. We were also facing an eviction – courtesy of our anti-wind friends. Sam was four or five by then and needed to go to school if we were staying in the same place.

Besides, Enercon would come visit me in Britain before long: I needed a better set-up. It was this confluence of factors that led to a big moment in my life – the reversal of that pivotal decision ten years earlier to go live on the road. I needed to move from living on the road to living in a house. We rented one nearby.

Sam had never lived in a house in his life.

He ran through the front door super-excited. It was a new-build, small terraced house. There was a toilet on the ground floor in a room the size of a cupboard and another one upstairs – and running water. We'd never had a toilet and now we had two. He ran from one to the other.

I found it difficult to begin with, living in a house. I was used to sleeping with the window open, keeping an ear out – but there was so much noise in town. I got used to that in time. I felt like I'd sold out to some extent and it grated on me living in a house. It was a bit twee, we had some stuffy neighbours (one of the great things about travelling is you actually do get to choose your neighbours) and I didn't like it much at all. It wasn't me. But it had its advantages and I spent my days making and installing masts and organising things from a little office in town. I just got on with it.

It was a great piece of happenstance, bumping into Enercon just as they were looking overseas – our interests were aligned. We got on well and it suited us both to do this. It came about through persistence and ultimately good old door knocking. And the timing was good, that always helps. It was early days. We helped each other get a foothold in Britain.

I gave this new entity the obvious name – Enercon UK. And it put me at the heart of this revolutionary technology, and started what was to become a great partnership and friendship. We went on to build a series of Enercon machines, and demonstrated them to an audience of industry, planners, public and government. These machines had distinct advantages – not least of which were low noise and the slow speed they rotated at. They also had grid benefits because the electricity was made suitable for the grid by new power electronics – you could pretty much choose the characteristics you needed and they supported weak grids rather than adding to their burden. In this respect, these machines were digital in an analogue age.

For an operator, they were mechanically simple, with an expected longer lifespan. And more productive in any given wind, but especially in low-windspeed areas – which is where we chose to build.

As I write this we've built a generating capacity of nearly 100 megawatts with Enercon across all four home countries of the UK and some in Ireland.

The most prominent of our Wind Parks (as we like to call them) was built at Green Park, Reading in 2005, right alongside the M4. It's the most visible windmill in Britain by far. It was a deliberate choice of location: we wanted to put a big windmill where people could see it and judge for themselves. Most people back then still hadn't seen one. I drove down the M4 the day after we built it and was mildly horrified that the whole six lanes, both directions of traffic, had slowed to an almost standstill as people rubber-necked this gigantic new windmill. We painted our name on the tower in huge letters, as was our way back then. And sat back and let people see and judge for themselves.

In the early days with Enercon I spent a lot of time at their factory. We identified the new gearless E-40 as the machine we would build in Britain. It wasn't quite ready but nor were we. One day Juanita (my good friend there) said we needed a manual for it, for the operator. I hadn't thought about that – I assumed there would be one, maybe in German and we could translate it, but there wasn't. I got the job of writing it – which was perfect. I needed to know how to operate this machine once we built the first in Britain, Enercon needed one anyway, for others – it also better qualified me to talk to industry types about our windmills and how they worked. I spent a few weeks at the factory in Germany crawling over part-assembled machines, getting drawings from the engineering teams, creating illustrations, translating technical German words (I love them) into English – writing this from an operator's point of view. Always asking myself the question, 'What do I need from a handbook to operate this machine?'

So the first manual for this first-of-a-kind machine was thus written in English and translated into German. Later again, it was translated into Indian. I lost track after that. I tweaked the book to cover the later E-30 model, which was designed for the Indian market. One of the tests we needed to do, well my good friend Marcus and I told ourselves we needed to do, was climb to the top of a working E-30 prototype and throw the emergency stop button. You know, to make sure the book was right. The tower rocked wildly from side to side as the machine came to a rapid stop. We hung on (were strapped on), expecting it, but no less excited by the actuality. Wind energy was always fun.

Later we abseiled off of our machine at the Ecotech Centre, some crazy dudes base-jumped from it – 70 metres to the ground with a parachute. Before that, I jumped off our first mill at Nympsfield, at our open event, to abseil down, learning a vital lesson for the future – best to turn the windmills first.

That windmill has a concrete tower – a feature of those is their narrowness, so narrow there's no room for a ladder inside the tower (there is no inside the tower, in fact). You climb up a ladder attached to the outside and then, at the top (where the tower is not much wider than the ladder), get on to a platform that circles the tower top – like a crow's nest. So I set off, my first abseil (it's quite hard to let go and trust the rope), our opening event; we had music and food and bands in a mini-festival below and as I descended someone taking pictures encouraged me to push away from the tower further, for more drama. I did that, but as I swung back in missed the tower with my feet and sailed past – not quite far enough to meet the blades passing on the other side of the tower, but close. Very close. So after that we adopted a simple rule – turn them off before jumping.

The third business was created to hold our wind development blueprint and apply it to more projects – this was Next Generation, the company through which we built all of our subsequent windmills and, later, other green energy projects.

Most developers chased wind more than any other factor, this led the focus of early developments to the high ground in England and into conflict with various protection groups – it created the fundamental conflict (and artificial choice) that still exists between wind energy and the landscape. We pursued a different route: we didn't chase high windspeed and remote, exposed, controversial locations. Instead, we looked for reasonable wind but closer to the grid and to roads – we balanced lack of wind with lack of cost for grid and roads, and relative lack of planning adversity. And we were aided in that by our technology choice. Gearless variable speed machines beat everything in these conditions. Our first project was 1,500 metres from the grid – that was short for the industry. Our second project was 100 metres from the grid. And despite being a monster, it got planning permission at the first time of asking.

We pioneered the use of wind in these locations and built the first windmills in a host of English regions as a result – getting windmills in front of more people was important to us. And we built on industrial sites to power big industry users, like Sainsbury's, Ford and the Prudential, where we operated in a new way – off-grid in effect. Here we traded lower winds for higher end-user value – and no losses in the delivery of the power. We made the power where it was used.

I set out to build a windmill, without a plan beyond that. Our first business was born of necessity – our need for a mast. The second with Enercon was more happenstance. The third was Next Generation, our green energy development arm – and that was just a matter of organisation, of pragmatism, putting all the stuff we'd learned into one place so we could repeat the process. The fourth, which I was yet to launch, was necessity again – replacing the middlemen to reach the end user with our new kind of power.

This is how we built the group that makes up Ecotricity today. Or rather how it came to be.

Much later we would do something very different – this time through serendipity.

CHAPTER 8
A BIT OF A JOKE

In 1995, the year before we built that first windmill, I could see the day coming and my thoughts turned to building more.

To do that we needed a fair price for the power. It was a key but missing ingredient. So I went to see the local power company (the MEB), the same one that had been so difficult over the grid connection for our first mill. That problem was solved, and now I went to talk to them about a new kind of electricity – the green kind.

They laughed at the idea. Literally. It wasn't an uncommon reaction. Nor were the things they said uncommon – what's green electricity and who's going to want it anyway?

That didn't bother me; I reasoned that green electricity didn't exist so how could people want it? In any event, I would make them want it. I was convinced that green energy was such a great idea that once people saw it was possible they would want it.

No, those reactions weren't the problem – it was this one.

The MEB was the only company we could sell our power to. They were one of the 12 state-owned energy companies that had been sold off – privatised in 1990. But they owned the entire regional network for electricity supply – it was a natural monopoly. These 12 entities competed with each other to supply energy in each other's areas, but had to pay each other to use the local wires that each of them owned – some weird kind of free market, that. Twelve public monopolies turned into 12 privately owned companies with local monopolies.

Anyway, the rules of the game back then were that if you generated electricity at the local level the only people you could sell it to were these local grid companies, the people that owned the local network – in our region the MEB.

The MEB knew this and they behaved like monopolists, basically saying to me, 'You can only sell it to us and here's a rubbish price.'

I left that meeting clear in my mind that to get a fair price for green energy in order to build more windmills, I needed to reach the end user with it – I had to cut out this middleman.

We needed to become an energy company.

The energy industry hadn't just been privatising, it was liberalising also – they were different things, as liberalisation allowed competition, and brought new rules to enable that.

So, thanks to Thatcher (and the irony of that is not lost on me) in the early nineties it became possible to become an independent electricity supplier. I decided that's what we had to do next. Like the windmill decision before it, it came without knowing what was involved – I was simply certain that it could be done, and that it had to be.

I formed a company for the purpose and named it the Renewable Energy Company. It was a joke. The name itself did describe us quite perfectly, but at the same time it gave us significant initials.

Most of the 12 previously state-owned energy companies kept their original names but they were also known as Regional Electricity Companies and by the acronym REC.

Our new company was also an REC, that was our joke, and we were the thirteenth (a favourite number of mine as it happens). It was a challenge to the industry; we were far smaller of course, but we pulled the tiger's tail – for fun. And actually it became our handle in the energy settlement system – we were REC13.

It was an insider's joke, from outsiders who set up to sell something that itself was not being taken seriously – green energy. Green energy is energy made from renewable sources, like the wind or the sun, rather than from burning fossil fuels. There are nuances to that: less green forms of energy that are presented as green that I would consider pale green, like from Landfill gas. And those which I don't consider green at all, like waste to energy because it involves burning rubbish and depends on rubbish creation … hardly sustainable.

Getting a licence was easy, as easy as faxing a few pages of information to the industry regulator Ofgem. There were no systems required, no money in the bank or anything. Which was just as well.

Over the next year I spent some time looking at Britain's energy system and how we could make this work, along the way coming up with a new way to supply energy, using the local grid and avoiding the national one – supplying local power to local customers. This suited the nature of renewables: small and decentralised.

It wasn't possible at the outset but became so as this period coincided with the emergence of another new opportunity in the industry and new rules – the National Grid's non-pooled generation scheme. This scheme was to start on 1 April 1996. Lots of events in energy start on April Fool's Day. That became our first day of supplying electricity as REC, using this new ability to match local customers to local generators.

The idea of embedded generation was out there already, generators connected to local grids (as opposed to national) – we added to this the concept of embedded supply. It had economic advantages: by avoiding the use of the National Grid we avoided the use of system charges and system losses involved in that.

You can think of the National Grid as a series of motorways which you pay a toll to use. Each motorway junction gets you on to a network of smaller roads. In electricity this is the territory of the local grid companies (the RECs) – if we operated within one of these we avoided the national tolls and paid only the local ones, and only incurred local losses too, this was an issue of efficiency as well as economics.

Liberalisation allowed us to become an energy company and enabled us to break the monopoly of the local grid companies and sell local generation to local people. And in the process offer a new kind of energy – the green kind.

Our first customer was Cheltenham and Gloucester College, our first generator was a landfill site in the same area, from which we bought 'green' energy. Not the most ideal form, but given that landfill created methane that needed flaring and or leaked into the atmosphere (where it's 30 times more potent as a greenhouse gas than CO_2), making energy with it was on balance a good thing to do. We set out a vision of deep and pale green energy sources at that time. We were the first people to sell this new kind of electricity, the green kind, anywhere in the world.

Shortly after us, a year or two later a company called Green Mountain started up in the US, and in Britain SWEB (the South Western Electricity Board), one of the newly privatised entities, entered the game with a tariff they called Green Electron. Green electricity grew from there to the global movement it is today.

A year after we completed that first windmill, almost to the day, I found myself at the event where the world first set legally binding carbon reduction targets.

It was another key moment that came out of nowhere when I got the chance to go to Kyoto in December 1997 for the United Nations climate change event.

The United Nations Framework Convention on Climate Change (UNFCCC) had begun in 1992 – its founding premise was that climate change was real and most likely caused by manmade CO_2 emissions (it actually says 'extremely likely', that's how long this has been known with such certainty). The Kyoto meeting was to build on this.

It established the first international treaty to reduce greenhouse gases, and pretty much the whole world signed up to it.

A friend of mine (Christophe) worked at the EWEA (European Wind Energy Association). He'd got some tickets on short notice for this UN gig. Another friend (Nick) ran the BWEA (British Wind Energy Association) – the idea was the three of us would go.

We'd found ourselves in interesting positions in this new industry, but didn't take ourselves seriously. We were irreverent, fun-loving types, but pursuing something we believed in. I have no idea how Christophe got the passes – but it felt like something that might be interesting and useful. We would go there and lobby for the role of wind energy in the world's emerging climate change plans. And have some fun.

In UN jargon this was COP 3 (Conference of the Parties number 3) – right at the start of it all. As I write this COP 26, due to be held in Britain in 2020, has been cancelled because of a different crisis – the virus one. I didn't know much about COPs or the UN at that time – I mean, I knew about the cops of course, but not COPs.

COP 3 turned out to be a historic event; the world agreed its first legally binding carbon reduction targets. We played no part in that, just to be clear. We were operating, I would say, anarchically, on the fringe, bending the ears of any and all delegates that we could about the role of wind energy. Exploring and partying in the evenings.

I took some windmill brochures and we set up a small table in the lobby and just talked to people. I was surprised to see the nuclear industry with a well-organised presence, arguing even then that nuclear energy was a low-carbon source and part of the answer.

The longest flight I'd been on by then was to Germany, to visit Enercon. This one was a monster trip, and I remember eventually emerging out of that plane into fresh air and big relief.

We caught the train to Kyoto. Nick had spent time in Japan and spoke some Japanese so he kinda was like our in country guide. Christophe was au fait with the UN and was our guide to that world. I was the green energy guy.

We ate in traditional places, drank sake and went to an amazing event thrown by our hosts, with traditional drumming (big sticks on tree-trunk-sized drums in the style of a martial art) and did a bit of dress-up. They opened some special barrels of sake and we were all given a keepsake – a traditional square wooden sake cup. It's the oddest thing to drink from – like a miniature Japanese bath really. I've lost mine sadly. But not my taste for sake.

The conference lasted a few days. We read the news and heard the gossip on the ground, saw John Prescott arrive and witnessed this historic event: the long night of negotiation and the news the next morning that 150 nations had signed up and it was on.

My two friends needed to leave – I needed to stay. I'd spotted an exhibition for electric vehicles to which I just had to go. Waiting for that, I spent a couple of days in the country all alone – that was a thrill.

Talk about stranger in a strange land. There wasn't much English speaking to be found, so my ears were listening to music, the cadence and tone of the spoken word – with no obvious meaning, no lyrics.

More impactful was the written language. It meant nothing to me. Normally I'm distracted, bothered by signs, adverts, words in windows and on trucks. I see it all, read it all and it affects me – I can't not think about it. In Japan everything I saw made no sense at all; it was liberating. I was adrift in a world where nothing that I heard or saw meant anything. I loved it. It was like tuning out.

The targets coming out of Kyoto were small, a 5 per cent cut in emissions, and didn't kick in for a decade – the treaty got a mixed reaction back home. Many people thought it was too little. I didn't see it that way – getting most of the world to accept climate change was real and manmade was a big deal. However small the initial targets were, this was a massive step.

Even the US signed up – though they would later drop out.

I was excited to go to the electric vehicle show. Cars were a big part of the problem and the idea of electrifying them was pretty radical.

There weren't any in the world that I had seen. I was a little disappointed to find there was only one at the show! That's how rare they were. It was a RAV4 that had been modified by Toyota, with an electric motor and a lot of car batteries (the old lead acid type). Still, it was exciting; I wanted to get one, but couldn't persuade them. They were running a very small trial on an island and that was it.

While I was there a Japanese guy approached me and offered me a small book. He held it out in both his hands in the traditional way and a lady nearby told me what he was saying, more or less. This was a book of his poetry, handwritten, and he wanted me to have it. I was moved by that. I couldn't read it, of course, but it was a really touching moment.

I left the show for the journey home – it would be another 13 years before Ecotricity would launch its own electric car, the wind-powered supercar we dubbed the Nemesis.

And before the worldwide electrification of cars began.

As I flew home at the end of 1997, our first windmill was one year old and at 40 metres tall, still the largest in Britain as well as the first of this new type. We were working on plans for the next two or three as Next Generation, our newly formed development arm – where all of our experience and the blueprint from the first project sat.

In two more years we would establish another significant milestone for wind energy in Britain with the first megawatt-scale machine. At that time the industry was facing intensifying opposition from the Country Guardians and felt great angst about windmill size. There was uncertainty about the wisdom of going bigger than the current norm, which was 30 metres high and less than half a megawatt of power.

We broke the spell at Swaffham in Norfolk with our second windmill: a 1.5 megawatt, 70-metre-tall piece of moving art. We added a viewing platform at the top and opened the first and – for decades – only windmill in the world open to the public to climb. It was a potent combination. We needed to demonstrate megawatt-class machines and there is no better demonstration than being able to go see and hear one – except being able to climb one. It had a spiral staircase inside the tower and a glass and steel circular viewing gallery at the top designed by Sir Norman Foster. Environment minister Michael Meacher opened it for us that October.

I never set out to create or lead a group of companies. All of this has been an organic process. Like the process of building that first windmill, taken one step at a time. Each challenge led to another solution and sometimes another company – first Western Windpower, the Enercon collaboration, then Next Generation, then REC. Others came later – but never out of a grand design, often out of happenstance, frequently out of necessity. Sometimes serendipity. Going with the flow in many ways, swimming against the tide in others.

We've grown from an idea to build one windmill, to do something to tackle the climate crisis, evolved to be a new kind of energy company, tackling energy as the biggest single cause of climate change. And then we looked further – adding the second and third biggest sources, transport and food, to our mission. And so began to evolve an approach that was all encompassing – a path to zero emissions. Rooted in the doable, not theory. Our roots are in doing stuff not talking about it – our picture of what needs to be done is grounded in what we have done and can see can be done.

Operating as a business was a conscious choice. Back when the green energy supply idea was forming, I thought there were two ways to present this new kind of energy: as a good cause that people should support, something that was worthy – or as a product that they could buy on competitive terms. I figured the business proposition had longer legs. And business itself has some good aspects – the organisation around an aim (unfortunately usually profit) and the efficiency of operation – compared to your average charity. What was needed, I reckoned, was a business that was mission-led, not profit-led, that had an environmental objective and used the tools of business to deliver it. A hybrid, part-NGO, part-business – taking the best of each.

In our earliest communications about the Renewable Energy Company we described ourselves as 'environmentalists doing business, not a business doing the environment'. This was an important distinction for us: even back then greenwashing by businesses was out there – less so than it is today, but it was there. And the eco-minded people we would appeal to first were switched on to this issue. As were we.

Another early message and founding aim was to supply 'green energy for the price of brown' and 'energy that didn't cost the earth'. We pushed 'the power to choose' to highlight that people had the power actually to choose who supplied their energy and thereby where it came from. Our message has been about people power from the beginning and the power of choice.

We adopted our own language to describe ourselves: a not-for-dividend company – the money we make goes back into our mission, not to shareholders. As a company we follow the 'eat to live' philosophy. Put another way, we make money for the mission: our mission is not to make money.

Capitalism got us into this mess. The rampant burning of fossil fuels that has created the climate crisis has been driven more than anything else by the current version of capitalism – which you might think off as the Thatcher version, the every-person-for-themselves, dog-eat-dog version. Along the way, capitalism like this has driven us to the verge of the sixth great extinction, into the Anthropocene era – a new geological epoch defined by human impact and created all the social ills of the world, not the least of which was slavery, let's not forget that.

But I think business has a vital role to play in solving these problems. We need to repurpose capitalism, make it work differently, make it seek better outcomes than just money and especially money at all costs. It's more than possible – we've been doing it for a quarter-century now, as have others.

Business is effective at getting things done. The rules and laws around business are not like the laws of physics – they are manmade. We can make them how we want them to be (someone already has). For too long we've been in thrall to the narrative of free markets and the idea that the profit motive is the single magic ingredient to life, the thing that ensures a good outcome, that wealth creation that way helps us all.

The rules of our economy and society and tax system are likewise manmade – poverty isn't a law of nature, it's a law of man – the by-product of an economic system that prioritises wealth, its accumulation and retention over the wellbeing of us all.

We live in a dog-eat-dog world but the rules of the game embed advantage, privilege and disparity – it's not an equal fight. Why do we tax money made with money at a lower rate than we tax money made with a pair of hands? Why do companies pay lower rates of tax than ordinary working people? These are examples of a system that values wealth and enables it's retention. We don't have to accept that as normal – it's not communist (despite what my parents used to think many years ago) to think we can do this differently.

The US is an extreme example, the UK a shadow of that. The EU pulls in another direction.

Social outcomes matter as much as environmental ones and in both cases – more than making money. Making money should not be the be all and end all of life, of our economy and the entities that exist within it.

We need to eat to live. It's a choice.

CHAPTER 9
NO BIG DEAL

It was a big deal.

About a year after the trip to Kyoto we started a joint venture with Thames Water.

It took most of that year to sketch out and then negotiate. It was something special, complex and entirely new.

At the heart of it was a contract to supply electricity to all of their sites (they had several hundred). We would supply them straight from the Pool at wholesale prices, with a small added margin – I think it was 2 per cent.

Electricity was one of their biggest overheads and this gave them access to the lowest possible prices – it was a big deal for them, saved them a lot of money. It was a big deal for us too: they used over £100,000 worth of electricity every day.

The Pool was a key part of the energy supply system, created to enable privatisation in 1990. Essentially it was the wholesale market – it was artificial and imperfect as all markets are to one degree or another. All generators sold to the Pool and all suppliers bought from the Pool. Prices were the same for everybody and set each day in advance.

The mechanism for price setting was probably its biggest flaw. Generators bid to supply the next day, the Pool chose the cheapest bid first until it had all the power that it needed, then bizarrely paid everyone on that list the same price, the price of the last bid in – the highest. That left it open to gaming and (even without gaming) kept prices higher than they needed to be, clearly, as most generators were paid more than they bid.

The Pool was replaced as part of a market reform in 2001 when the New Electricity Trading Arrangements (NETA) came into force – which added to the challenge we faced in this part of our story.

As a supplier we had access to the Pool and its wholesale prices, and we passed those on to Thames. A crucial element of the deal was they had to pay us daily for the power because we had to pay the Pool daily – we didn't have the cash to support the amount Thames used for any period of time. Later, they would try to use this against us.

They would also pay us monthly for all of the costs of delivery, Transmission and Distribution (national and local) charges, again at pass through.

Normally power was wrapped up into a bundled price, without transparency of the many elements, and made more expensive that way. This was a big departure.

The whole deal with Thames took our turnover to about £50 million a year – three years earlier, in our first year we had a turnover of £13,000 – so it was a colossal step in that respect. And we were still only about a dozen people big.

I went to a utilities conference in the Netherlands soon after to speak on the subject of green energy. The other utilities there were presenting thoughts about what might be possible with green energy – we were there to talk about what we were doing already and we'd just arrived at this massive turnover. We surprised everybody there. We were streets ahead.

Thames also made green electricity themselves, using sewage. Part of the deal was a joint venture, a new company that would supply green energy, starting with the green energy that Thames made themselves. We named it the New Power Company – it was a Ronseal thing.

We ran this new company, contracted with Thames to buy all of their green energy, sold it to business users, did the billing and so on in a facsimile of what we did at the Renewable Energy Company. Thames liked our model and wanted to play.

At that time we were supplying to all businesses, however large or small, but not yet to homes.

We were also planning to buy green energy from other generators for this new company. At launch the biggest of those was London Waste – as the name suggests they made power from waste collected in London. Thames were keen to have this energy, we were not – it wasn't on our list of deep or pale green sources. But for Thames it was an opportunity to further reduce their energy bills. They underwrote a contract for our tiny new company to buy this massive amount of power produced by London Waste, guaranteeing the multimillion-pound annual cost. As a large user, Thames provided the fallback demand to absorb this power – and so the new joint venture would also supply Thames that way.

We launched the Thames deal early in 1999 with the help of John Battle, the energy minister. We said all the grand things you do at launches – talked of how it was like the beginning of a new world, and it felt like it was. I took Sam out of school for the day. We caught a train to London, spent the night before at the launch venue – the hotel next to where the London Eye is now. It was a big event – not the launch, I mean the whole thing that we were doing.

It's hard to describe just how exciting this time was. The world had just agreed its first binding emissions targets, and we'd seen green energy go from a crazy idea nobody believed in just a few years ago, to this. It felt like the big time and it had happened in no time.

Thames got big savings on their bills, they got to be a part of a green energy supply company and get better prices for their own generation. We made a small percentage on a large bill, gained access to relatively vast amounts of green energy, and got a massive boost to our credibility and that of our concept – green energy. We were both winners, as the best deals require.

The negotiations had been tough. The power-supply element was straightforward enough, the interaction of the numerous contacts made for complexity – but the biggest problem was the New Power Company itself. Thames were insistent on forming this new supply company and I couldn't see a good reason for that, only suspicious ones. The contract negotiations confirmed that outlook.

We had many meetings lasting many hours to thrash out the details and the deal seemed to grow more complex the more we met. Thames always had a big team, six to eight people, directors and lawyers, and we were a team of two – me and our lawyer Julia. We worked hard to avoid onerous terms, being stitched up.

Things came to a head over the new supply company. Finally, exasperated with all that they wanted, I told them that if their plan was one day to set up themselves to be a power company, if one day we would face them in the market – then we would rather do that now than help them by building this company that they could one day take from us. It was a turning point. My mind was made up. I collected my papers together and got ready to leave. Julia told me afterwards that she thought I was actually leaving. Thames saw it that way too. It broke the impasse. We signed shortly after.

Groundbreaking is a bit of a cliché – but this deal was nothing if not that. This stuff hadn't been done before. And although we had a really complex set of contracts, we had a deal and an opportunity to make it work.

And for a while, it did.

We took responsibility for their entire electricity account and our turnover hit £50 million. Numbers like that put us on the map – it gave enormous credibility to our work, the things we said and to this new concept – green energy. That's what big numbers can do.

We were so very busy behind the scenes keeping up with data flows, billing and the admin, all using spreadsheets; we had no billing systems, no systems worthy of the name. We had to learn a lot and we had to learn it fast. And we had to do it well: Thames were demanding.

Thames introduced us to the people running the Millennium Dome and they became a customer. We supplied them in the run up to the millennium and then for that one year of operation as an attraction in 2000. We did this all with green energy from sewage in London, including from the Dome itself, and the joke of the moment was that if you flushed a loo at the Dome the lights got brighter. It was a fantastically high-profile customer to have, shame we struggled to get paid, eventually having to threaten insolvency proceedings …

We missed the launch party – the big turn-of-the-millennium event as 1999 rolled into 2000. As a key partner we thought we might get tickets but Thames told us there weren't any. Later, we learned this was a lie – there had been and they kept them for themselves. We found this out as part of the disclosure process of the later court action. Disclosure has proven to be a very powerful tool for us in unearthing deceit and putting right wrongdoing. We would use it again on other corporate bad actors.

But at this stage it was all systems go – we picked up a Millennium Products award from Tony Blair that year and won a Queen's Award for the Environment. It felt like we and our ideas had arrived. Just before that, we'd been invited to take part in the Lord Mayor's Show, had a float built for us and took pretty much our whole team to London for the event. We were about the size of a football team.

It was later in 2000 when it started to go pear-shaped. Pool prices became volatile and Thames were exposed to the other side of buying straight from the market – prices went up sometimes.

Saving a whole bunch of money looked like a great idea in 1998; come the early 2000s Thames had lost their energy expert and market exposure was being seen by their board more as a risk. It wasn't a fundamental increase in price – that had been falling since 1998 – it was more of a blip, the kind of thing that evened out over a year. But Thames didn't want to deal with it. They couldn't budget for it. They wanted price certainty, which is what a bundled price gives you.

We were called to a meeting and knew it was a make-or-break thing.

The night before I went out for a curry with Kate in Stroud. I'd just been to the dentist and had my bridge removed and replaced with a temporary one. This bridge was a set of six teeth at the front and top of my mouth – a legacy of my bike crash about 20 years earlier. It was very difficult to have made and fitted back in the day, and had become hard to live with. But then it had done well, lasting 20 years, 10 of those on the road. Dentist tech had moved on massively – the original took months and many visits to make and to perfect. In one visit it was prised off and a temporary version made and fitted; I was good to go while they made a permanent version out of porcelain and white gold. This temporary version was plastic, and the one thing the dentist stressed to me was this: don't eat spicy food because it would stain.

We went to a curry house – don't ask me why.

I remember eating dahl and thinking if I kept it away from my front teeth (it's not like you need to bite or chew dahl) I could get away with it. But as we prepared to leave the curry house that night Kate looked at me funny and told me my teeth looked a bit yellow.

When we got home I looked in the mirror with better lighting and was horrified: my front teeth were luminous yellow and I was about to meet with Thames the next day. It was a crunch meeting, they needed to have confidence that we knew what we were doing and I was going to turn up with luminous yellow teeth – it was like a nightmare or some crazy comedy sketch. Except it was actually happening. I rang the number the dentist had given me for emergencies and incredibly she came out at midnight and did some surface grinding to remove the top layer of yellowness – it was the turmeric that had done it. She reminded me I had been warned. Super dentist, Dr Roz.

I got to the meeting in Reading without looking batshit crazy. We did our best to reassure them. We couldn't tell if we had; it was clear they were under big pressure and this deal was being scrutinised and judged. It hung in the balance.

Not long after, a team from Thames came to meet at our place. The directors we usually dealt with had brought someone more senior with them, a guy I'd met when we signed the deal – he didn't get involved day to day. By then we were based by the train station in Stroud in an old building society HQ, complete with a strong room – it had a lot of character, that place. We had a meeting room upstairs with a huge circular wooden table, which could seat 12 people; it's how we liked to meet, at a round table – there's something very balanced about that.

It's fair to say that it was a difficult meeting. But there was no conclusion, just lots of questions and uncomfortableness.

At the end, the boss guy asked if he could have a word with me in private and we went into my office downstairs. We didn't sit down: this wasn't going to take long it seemed. He told me they wanted out of the contract. It was as simple as that. I said that was fine, not really a surprise, we'd been getting that impression – the contract had exit provisions, ways for either of us to leave. But he said to me, 'No, we're breaking the contract. And if you stand in our way, we're going to break you too.' Just like that.

He gave me a list of things they wanted – information, assignment of contracts, payments, all sorts of stuff – within 24 hours or something just as crazy, and said we had to give them everything they wanted and they would decide what, if anything, they would let us have. This was not remotely ever going to happen.

I told him we'd insist on following the contracts and would go to court if we had to. It was suddenly that kind of conversation. We had no problem ending things but it needed to be done properly, according to the terms of the contracts. That's what they were there for. Didn't seem unreasonable to me.

He looked at me; we were stood up and he was a tall guy, clearly he felt his own size, it was part of how he spoke to people, how he projected himself. He said, 'You won't get us to court because we'll bankrupt you before you can get there.'

And with that he left. I knew now why he wanted to speak in private. No witnesses.

There was never a question of not fighting them. It didn't matter to me if we lost and lost everything fighting this, I wasn't going to accept it – it was sheer badness.

So then it began.

We learned how Thames intended to break us straight away.

They stopped paying for their daily power use, over £100,000 a day. We had no way to stop paying for it ourselves, to the Pool, and so they reckoned to bankrupt us this way, in a matter of days – and they would have, had they not overlooked the rest of the joint venture.

But first we responded to this non-payment of bills with a threat to disconnect their electricity supply. They were shocked and aggrieved we would do this, in disbelief really, as was much of the industry – but them's the rules and we had no qualms. We started the process determined to fight fire with fire – sometimes I think you have to fight fire with napalm.

Our target for this action was their HQ in Reading. Not all 300 sites as reported in the press, just this one. It was the nerve centre of their operation and the most high-profile, most embarrassing target we could hit.

It was March 2001, about two years into the deal and about ten days into their attempts to break us, when the story hit the press. Thames's energy debt to us was already over £1 million and climbing – daily.

They were freaked out by the prospect, bleated about health and safety and anything else they could think of. Instead of just paying their energy bills they ran to the regulator Ofgem and asked them to intervene. It was hilarious. It was more drama than the utility industry ever saw and Thames were very much on the back foot.

Ofgem asked us to reconsider. We said we wouldn't, couldn't – we needed to be paid. Ofgem couldn't prevent us doing this so instead tried to broker a deal. Thames made them a promise that if we stopped the process of disconnection they would pay their bills. That was all we wanted so with Ofgem telling us they had these promises from Thames – what else were we to do? We believed it and halted the process.

But it was a lie: they did not resume payments, not then or ever. Ofgem did nothing about that, which lowered them in my estimation, as you can imagine.

Thames, meanwhile, were trying to switch their sites away from us to a new supplier, London Electricity – another of the privatised energy entities.

We took our case to the High Court and sought an urgent injunction against Thames to prevent them switching their sites to London Electricity – it was a clear breach of our contract. We won that and had a court date set for the following week. More PR and more embarrassment for them.

The hearing the next week was interesting. It gave me a first exposure (businesswise – I'd seen it as a traveller) to how the courts work, how judges operate and think, how the law works. We lost and we won.

The judge could see the jeopardy we were in and the contract we had – Thames had no way to counteract the clear fact that this would be a breach of contract, their arguments about that were risible. The judge said he sympathised with our position (saying something about wanting to protect the shorn lamb) but because we had a remedy through further legal action, we could sue them later and Thames were clearly big enough to pay compensation, the right course of action he felt was to let them carry on and for us to pursue a claim for breach of contract. That was disappointing but I could see the argument.

The argument I struggled to accept was the one made by Ofgem, who joined the proceedings as industry regulator, and basically argued that customers should be allowed to break energy-supply contracts. What kind of market were they trying to encourage?

The judge also said we had an 'arguable case' for breach of contract. In legal terms, this was significant – it blew a hole below the water line in Thames's position. They would very likely lose the subsequent case and be exposed to damages. All we had to do was to survive to have that day in court. The boss's words rang in my ears: you won't get us to court because we'll break you first.

But Thames had made a mistake. Maybe it was hubris, maybe it was the simple overestimation of their size versus ours, or maybe they didn't really understand our joint venture. Or maybe they just weren't that smart. I think that covers all possibilities ...

I watched a wildlife programme on TV once about a stickleback and a pike. I used to catch sticklebacks in the local dykes when I was a kid. I had an affinity for them. The stickleback didn't try to run from the pike, it wasn't likely to win that race – no, it sat squarely in front of the pike and let the bigger fish try to swallow it whole. The pike gulped it into its mouth, but the stickles on its back made it impossible for the pike to actually swallow the little fish – it had to spit it out. The stickleback sat calmly in front of the pike and allowed itself to be repeatedly swallowed and spat back out, until the pike eventually gave up. The pike had all the natural advantages of size, power and speed, but the stickleback had one thing: it couldn't be swallowed if it wasn't afraid. We were the stickleback and Thames were the pike – that's how I saw it – the perfect wildlife metaphor for what was happening. They made several attempts to swallow us, oblivious to our spikes perhaps. And eventually gave up.

The mistake that Thames made was to overlook the whole joint venture. They were focused only on the supply of energy to their sites, their energy bills. Meanwhile, they were supplying energy to us from their own generation – which we had stopped paying for. And even more significantly, we were being supplied by London Waste, with a huge volume of power, which Thames had to pay for if we didn't. We stopped paying for that too and Thames had to pay for all the energy we were receiving and trading. It was quite upsetting for them.

It was months before they twigged and could correct the situation – in that time, we'd accrued more money than they owed us. A lot more.

And because the court allowed them to switch their sites to London Electricity, they stopped racking up debts to us – that put an end to their first attempt to break us.

They demanded we paid them the generation money, of course, and we of course refused. Our court case against them for breach of contract was underway – these things take a long time, we expected three years, and this generation aspect would be washed out at that point. They couldn't get it to court sooner because it was all part of the same case. They were stuck. And we looked set to survive to get them into court.

A couple of years later, they reached out to negotiate a settlement to avoid the impending court date. It was what our lawyers said would happen. And it wasn't about what they had to pay us for breach of contract, as we'd turned the tables so effectively. It was about how much we were prepared to pay them. Which amused me.

The final settlement meeting was a lesson.

I believe Thames bugged us. We met in a hotel meeting room. They wanted to know how much money we were going to give them. They figured we owed them more for the energy we hadn't paid for than we had lost because of their breach of contract – which was at least arguably so. The calculations were complex and fraught with issues; there were lots of different sources of generation and differing possible values; different views on what we had lost on the one side, and how much we had gained on the other. I was playing with them, comfortable with our position, the impending court date, aware of their own discomfort and need to settle. I essentially said it doesn't matter how much you think we owe you – we don't have it. I wasn't bothered. They were frustrated and angry and the more they became so the more I had fun. The boot had very much changed foot.

Having exhausted efforts to impose their will on us and having told us the bare minimum sum they were willing to accept to settle the case, they offered to leave the room so that we could talk about it, Julia our lawyer and me. They left a briefcase on the table, conspicuously.

Julia talked about the legal position, I reiterated we had nothing to give them – it didn't matter what they wanted or who was right or wrong. I was suspicious of the way they had left, left us in the room with their case on the table, so

I maintained the same position as I had when they were in the room.

They came back in and ended the meeting, just like that. No further discussion. That raised my suspicions further. They didn't feel the need to ask if our view had changed.

Not long after that it settled, they came back to us and accepted our position. It was over. The pike had given up.

The sum we gained ultimately was never clear, it wasn't sat in a bank account, that part was true – my best guess was somewhere north of £3 million, might have been up to £5 million. The price of badness.

The same thing happened to us with Tesla many years later. We secured a high court injunction against them, learned much in the discovery process and eventually they wanted to settle before it got to court. They pulled the same stunt when we were talking about how much they should pay us. They said, 'We'll leave the room and let you talk about it.' I said it's OK we'll go – they were insistent that it was they who left. This was a hotel room that they had booked and were set up in when we arrived. And I'm convinced that they were listening in to our conversations. As with Thames I said what I wanted them to hear – I showed my ambivalence towards settling and picked a low number that I predicted they would come back in at. They did exactly that and I laughed out loud: this was no coincidence, I said so – they looked very uncomfortable.

The tech today is very different to the early 2000s, of course, making such a thing very easy to do. No briefcase needed.

So here is some advice from the guy that doesn't like to give advice, because this is specific: if you find yourself in a negotiation in a room someone else has prepared and they offer to leave to let you discuss among yourselves – don't do it. Either leave the room to talk or do as we did and stay in the room, saying only what you want them to hear.

At the start of the breakup with Thames, as well as the threat of bankruptcy, we were also facing a collapse in our turnover. The joint venture with Thames was perhaps 90 per cent of what we did. The prospect of that was daunting but the reality was the opposite; we found that we were happier and better off not being in this deal with Thames.

The other 10 per cent of our business was more fun and more worthwhile. Turnover isn't everything.

Losing Thames was no big deal.

For us it was a formative experience. An example of corporate badness and how that world operates, of how amoral the world of business can be. It would not be our last experience of this.

Refusing to accept such behaviour is instinctive. I know that it comes with the sort of risk that some people would not take. But I don't see it in those terms, as primarily a risk – I see it as fighting for the only thing that truly matters: principles. I'm unmoved by threats of loss or bankruptcy – that's not scary. When principles matter more than money – it's a red rag.

Somebody once said to me, in another situation, that it might be expensive to stand up for our principles in the way we intended. My response was if it's not expensive then they aren't principles. I believe that to be true. I've heard patents described as 'only as good as their first court case' – I understand why. And so it may be with principles they are only as good as their first test.

It's in my character to resist pressure. I can be persuaded but not pushed. It doesn't really matter what it is, whether it's the colour of my socks (school) or not wearing a tie (football), my hands in my pockets (courts) or whether I should just put up with badness – corporate badness in this case, I don't care what it is. It's not the right way to go about things. For me, injustice is a fundamental problem and one I always rail against. It's my nature.

Our battle with Thames was at its peak in March 2001 and the heat was out of it a few weeks later – though it rumbled on for years before settling. But we had other problems. The Pool was being replaced by NETA and to trade energy in this new world we needed systems and credit lines and functions we just didn't have.

In fact, these new arrangements were introduced the same month that we were attempting to disconnect Thames's HQ in Reading. That added to the ambiance.

We'd seen NETA coming, of course, and had found someone who could help us – TXU, another privatised entity and people we got on well with. By the introduction of NETA we'd made the transition to TXU for our energy trading issues.

So while wrestling with Thames on the one hand we'd negotiated this major system change with a new trading partnership. It was in this that Thames tried a different way to break us – knowing of our arrangement Thames Water got on the phone to TXU and tried to persuade them to drop us. It was a dirty move, suited them well.

TXU to their great credit refused to do so. The guys we worked with told us all about it. They'd been asked about the deal and said they liked what we were doing and wanted to work with us. That was enough and Thames failed again.

It was a busy time, but we weren't out of the woods.

TXU went bust. Just like that.

It was the autumn of 2002, a year and a half after NETA and the Thames drama began. TXU was one of the 12 privatised energy companies, with 5 million customers; going bust was never expected. But it was American-owned, the Enron scandal had hit hard and its parent company stopped funding it – it just went into administration one weekend.

And we suddenly had no ability to trade energy.

The administrators got in touch on the Monday and gave us until the end of the week to find a new trading partner or we were going to be thrown into the balancing market (huge daily penalties) and out of business. It was a severe situation to be in.

I reached out to the regulator, Ofgem, and asked them to help us get more time. The administrators wouldn't budge. But crucially Ofgem were in touch with the would-be buyer of TXU – Powergen. Yeah, another privatised entity. They were persuaded to give us one month to make other arrangements. That was still a very short timeframe, but better by far than one week.

The answer we found to this new challenge was more improbable than the bankruptcy of TXU. We bumped into a company in London that was shutting down. It was the energy trading arm of a big corporate entity, ABB. They weren't an energy supplier as we were – they traded energy as a commodity, bought and sold it as the price moved. They'd set this up presumably when things looked different in the energy market, and now they wanted out. But they had a problem. Some of their energy trades were two years into the future, if they cashed them out now they would crystallise big losses. We needed to trade energy, they needed to exit – but trade some energy.

There was a deal to be done. So we did one.

For a hundred quid we bought their entire trading operation.

In return we traded out the forward energy position for the parent company over the next two years and saved them a lot of money.

And you couldn't get more lock, stock and barrel than this deal. We got everything – their trading software (worth £1 million), computers, servers and desktops, the team of people that ran the operation, all the office equipment, even the furniture. We bunged it all in a van one weekend, brought it to Stroud and we set it all up to start trading the following Monday. Just in time.

Overnight we had a complete trading arm. To get one at all was amazing; to get one overnight, even more so; to get one overnight for one hundred quid . . . what can you say? It's beyond belief really. But it happened to us.

And of course it meant we survived the existential threat of TXU's bankruptcy. It was the greatest escape we've ever pulled off.

This new trading ability meant we had become a fully fledged energy company – it completed us and we no longer

More from the site in Scotland. The white out was bleak. We'd just got the mast up and were getting ready to leave.

Tim looking at our first mast, still on the ground, on the windmill hill in 1992.

Me, Brian and Tim (left to right) assembling that first mast in 1992.

Reading the local paper by the ex-air force trailer that was my last home on the road, on Brian's land in 1992.

Brian rolling a cigarette on that same day, Tim in his caravan, me hiding from the camera.

Me and Brian on his site later that day - there's a windmill on that pole behind me.

My son Sam, at the rear of our trailer in 1992.

Me and Sam inside our trailer in 1992. It was much nicer on the inside than the out...

Tim, Brian and me (left to right) on a local site doing a mast job in 1993.

The 4x4 lorry with a windmill attached to the crane – very quick way to put up a 20 foot tower. We were testing it here on Brian's land in 1994.

Me, standing in front of that first Windmill back in 1998.

The viewing platform being lifted to the top of Britain's first megawatt scale machine at the Ecotech Centre in Swaffham, 1999.

needed a partner to trade energy (a problem that the New Electricity Trading Arrangements caused – we were fine in the Pool days).

So in a few short years we'd navigated our way into a big deal with Thames, out the other side and through their various attempts to bankrupt us, through the end of the Pool and through the sudden market departure of TXU. It was a potent combination, an intense few years of multiple and overlapping threats – but as the great man said, what hadn't killed us had made us stronger.

We were one lucky stickleback.

In and out of big deals – impossible to swallow.

This is probably the most complex and challenging period of our story – the energy industry is both of these things, and it's been difficult to survive in it for one reason and another.

If I knew how hard this would be, how much time and energy it would take, back in 1995 I might not have started the Renewable Energy Company – that jokily named new entity and two fingers to the energy system. I'm glad that I did, but I think I may not have done so – had I known.

With the drama of Thames and TXU behind us, we were a fully fledged electricity company operating in the new market and things calmed down. Many years later we would battle with another bunch of corporate bastards also with T for an initial – but for now things were quiet.

We entered the domestic electricity market in 2003 – a long-held ambition.

One thing that's stood me in good stead, one ability I've had to hone is this; to be able to carry on with the small stuff amid great uncertainty, when facing problems that look intractable or for which there appears no answer – and thus not knowing if things will be OK, to be able to carry on in the face of that and make all the day-to-day decisions and future plans that still need making. Blanking out the risks and uncertainty, holding that at arm's length, and dealing with them as and when you can, is vital.

CHAPTER 10
ZEROCARBONISTA

My son Rui was born in 2008.

I have three sons, all 'brothers from another mother', as I once heard them say.

It was also the year of the global financial crash, when only massive state intervention saved the whole financial system from collapsing like a house of cards. We escaped relatively lightly with a big recession and a Conservative government, and though it impacted our views of banks, bankers and the whole system – calling much into question – ultimately little changed.

It did, however, lead directly to austerity, a political choice that gave us the 'lost decade' of brutal public sector cost-cutting and concomitant growth of that massive new third sector industry – food banks. We have the Tories to thank for that, and for the anti-green policies that were another hallmark of (David) Cameron, the husky hugger.

We were busy.

That year we introduced Zerocarbonista, launched the Greenbird, conceived the Nemesis, and built 21 more windmills.

Our work had begun in the nineties with a focus on energy because it was the biggest single source of carbon emissions in Britain and the biggest driver of climate change. It made perfect sense to start there.

Early in the new millennium we went looking for the second and third biggest sources of climate change – we'd made progress on the first, it was logical. We found them to be transport and food. And we discovered that energy, transport and food together make up about 80 per cent of a person's carbon footprint. That was an empowering revelation. It's underpinned our work since then.

Those three areas of life became our focus. We wanted to highlight the role that they played, individually and collectively. We wanted to explore a post-oil world, one where we tackled these issues – and through them climate change and the general unsustainability of life – with technology and behaviour change.

I believe the starting place is always information. Inform yourself or other people about the issues, the problems, and then what can be done about it. Without that structure or narrative, it makes less sense.

Our essential narrative was this: these three areas of life are in our own control. It's about how we power our homes, how we travel and what we eat – we all make decisions every day in these three walks of life. And because 80 per cent of our impacts are driven by these decisions – our decisions – we don't have to wait for governments and businesses to act: we have the power to bring about change. We all have that power.

It's a big picture view of the problem and an empowering view of our own role. Too often, I feel, we are bombarded with disconnected, often competing pieces of advice about what we should and shouldn't do to live greener lives and fight climate change. A lot of it seems trite – the media like to make it so. It's confusing and off-putting, and the scale of the problem, the climate crisis, itself makes it hard to see what any of us can do.

So we created Zerocarbonista and launched as a blog to put this world view out there and start conversations on these three essential areas of life and how we make the changes needed.

We launched with this paragraph: 'This blog is about answers to the big questions. How will we keep the lights on? What kind of cars will we drive? Will we drive at all? How will we feed ourselves in a post-oil world, and a world where we can't afford to keep burning things and throwing things away? Energy, Transport and Food are the three big issues.'

That year we began to look at transport – how we would all get about in a post-oil world. Cars were our gateway.

It started with a world record-breaking attempt using a car powered only by the wind. We named it the Greenbird in a nod to Donald Campbell and his Bluebird. What I didn't know at the time was that Donald Campbell hated the colour green and the number 13, and thought nothing good ever happened on a Friday – the polar opposite of my own views. Oh well.

The Greenbird smashed the wind-powered land speed world record a year later on 26 March 2009, on the dry bed of Ivanpah Lake in California, clocking 126mph. It was an amazing feat of engineering, designed by a British engineer

(Richard). This car could travel up to five times the speed of the wind that was propelling it.

I was a treehugger and a petrolhead, and I explored those contradictions on the blog. I needed a new car, and I wanted a green one, an electric one. Ideally a wind-powered one, but electricity could be the bridge.

There were none in the world, the Greenbird wasn't the kind of car you could drive on the road, so we decided to make one. How hard could it be right? My favourite self-deprecating kind of chirpy underdog expression from the nineties was, 'We've done more with less.'

We reached out to Lotus, who we knew from a project to build windmills at their site in Norfolk. We asked them if they were interested in making an electric car for us – surprisingly, they were. Using a Lotus made good sense; it was a small, lightweight platform and a cool car to look at. Beating the stereotype of electric cars that looked like milk floats was a front-and-centre consideration.

We got a long way with them and agreed a performance envelope that was possible at a reasonable cost – they knocked up some great images and we could see a path to doing this. But for some reason, we struggled to get to the end of negotiations and the start of the project. Eventually we gave up and went looking for another way to make it happen.

Not long after that, Lotus announced they had agreed to build electric cars for Tesla, the electric car company that Elon Musk had recently bought into and eventually took over (he's often cited as the founder but that's not correct), using converted Lotus models. And then we understood. The guys at Lotus told us they'd been holding back the deal with us because it would clash with this much bigger one they hoped to land. It was frustrating. We'd burned a lot of time with them.

Undeterred we'd found an ex-Lotus motor sport engineer, Jim, based in Norfolk, and started again. We set the car parameters like this – it had to do more than 100mph and do 0 to 60 in a handful of seconds; it had to look fantastic, handle fantastic and have a range of at least 100 miles. All of this was with an eye on the fact that electric cars didn't exist and we knew exactly how they would be received. We didn't want to make an electric car that was a compromise; in fact, we wanted to make an electric supercar. We didn't want a car that anybody reasonable would say 'yes but' about, at least as far as possible.

The weak link in our performance envelope was range. We set it at a 100-mile minimum based on typical car driving; 99 per cent of all car journeys in Britain were less than 100 miles and typical daily miles were closer to 10. In this respect, we had some persuading to do – we're all used to cars that can drive non-stop for 300 miles, even though it's (statistically) a rare thing to do. It was a trade-off: longer range needs bigger batteries, which means more weight.[1]

Jim assembled a team. To me they became the A-Team; that's how it felt, great characters and all specialists – and we got cracking.

We got hold of an old Lotus Exige on eBay and stripped it down, bought some electric motors and batteries pretty much straight out of R&D, but had to make our own battery management system – none existed at that time. That was the part that proved most difficult and took the longest.

Jim and his team knew the Lotus model we'd bought, the Exige. They knew its handling characteristics and the compromises that had been made – our car was going to handle better than the standard Exige in a straight line and round bends. No small thing given it's a very good car to start with and we were going to load it up with batteries – our car would weigh more.

The A-Team stretched our car, made it longer between the wheels and they lowered it and with it the centre of gravity. We engaged a top designer, Peter, to produce the look, modifying the front, creating a new rear, chopping off the roof and making it detachable. We finished it with a grey Union Jack paint job and hand-stitched seat covers with the lion and unicorn crest in Ecotricity green. It looked awesome.

It was a mad project, started in 2008 before there were any electric cars in the world that you could buy – I'd tried. We had nearly 300hp of electric motors crammed into the rear of the car with our own belt-drive reduction box and a battery containment system that was straight out of Formula 1. It was a Kevlar and carbon fibre container with cooling ducts and a fire suppression system; big red button in the cab – emergencies only. Lithium ion batteries were a relatively unknown quantity then.

But most importantly we were building a car to demonstrate how we could all be getting around in a post-oil world. We described this car as a wind-powered car, as we had with the Greenbird, but one you could drive on the road. For us it was to be powered by green electricity from the wind.

We filmed the making of this car, and broadcast on Zerocarbonista – aiming originally for six episodes and ending eventually on episode number 13, much later than we hoped. But this car worked; it drove straight out of the workshop, a rare thing for a brand new car, the A-Team told me.

We named it the Nemesis, partly inspired by a character in *2000 AD* (a comic from my travelling days) and partly because we saw this kind of car as the nemesis of internal combustion cars.

We had a glitzy launch in London; Damon Hill, a former F1 World Champion, joined us, and later we took it for a spin around Silverstone. That was an experience. We chatted away like we might have been driving to the supermarket, or at least he did; I found it slightly more exciting. We slid and screeched our way round every corner, hammered out of each bend, hard on the brakes into the next one. We needed all new brakes after that, they weren't up to the job, but Damon was always in complete control. It was special.

We got the Nemesis on the road in 2010, two years after we started. Lotus by then were adapting one of their models for Tesla and flying the cars to the US to have batteries fitted. Some would fly back to the UK again for sale – those cars had a high carbon footprint at birth. Nissan entered the game with the Leaf, a very sensible, practical car. Things were moving.

By this time we could see that the major motor manufacturers were already either making electric cars or planning to. The electric car revolution we'd hoped to foment was beginning.

We were looking for our next move. With car makers entering the game we felt we were no longer needed in that space – this was something they were best placed to do. Our best work, the place where we can make the most difference, is on the edge of things pushing boundaries, because we can. One of our unique abilities, stemming from our mission-led approach and not-for-dividend philosophy, and the source of our independence, is that we can choose to do things without considering commercial outcomes. We look for scalability though.

Electric cars, for example, had to be possible for everyone, not just a niche few – and so on Zerocarbonista we researched and shared findings on the big questions. Is there enough lithium in the world for all the world's cars to be electric? Could the National Grid take it – if all 30 million cars in Britain were electric? We found the answer was yes. Scalability is key when choosing what to pursue – we need mass adoption to achieve global change.

Our experience of having the Nemesis on the road led us to understand that having somewhere to charge was a big deal. It was the next frontier. We could see a classic chicken-and-egg stand off – people were reluctant to buy electric cars because there was nowhere to charge, and nobody wanted to build chargers with so few cars on the road.

We broke that impasse with the Electric Highway, a national network of chargers, or electricity pumps as we prefer to see them. We got started in 2011; it was Britain's first national charging network. As far as we could see it was the first in the world. We could see the need.

I've often been told that 'if something was that easy somebody would have done it already'. I think that's a lazy analysis – by definition somebody has to do everything for the first time. It's illogical to think something can't be done because it's not been done before.

We often find ourselves doing something that hasn't been done before. To me it's more of a sign we're on the right track, in the right place – applying ourselves where we can have the most impact.

Our focus for the Electric Highway was motorways, our reasoning was that this was where refuelling would be most needed, and that enabling long journeys was the key to mass adoption and to tackling the new concept of 'range anxiety'. We later expanded to include A-roads (especially in regions with no motorways) and covered off Land's End and John o'Groats; it's an iconic road trip and we hoped to take the Nemesis on that one day (back in the day when that would've been newsworthy in an electric car), but we never did. Our mission was to enable people with electric cars to be able to travel the length and breadth of the country.

My earliest recollection of environmental concern was when I was aged maybe 13, biking from school one day. I imagined all the cars on the road, reckoned they all had 10-gallon tanks, more or less, tried to imagine how much fuel that was in total and where it all came from. It seemed obvious to me that it had to run out, had to be finite – but nobody was talking about it. This was the early seventies. Compared to today, of course, there were nowhere near as many cars on the road.

In building the Nemesis I'd joined the dots on that boyhood concern, built an answer to that problem and other problems that I'd become aware of since, like air pollution, climate change – stuff like that.

The Nemesis had to be a great car. My view, informed by my experience, is that whenever you set out to do something in a different way, a green way, you have to do it really well – to avoid the 'yes but' trap. Consider an organic football pitch; it has to be a great surface to play on, among the best in any given league. Food is the same; food without animals in it is perceived to have something missing so it has to be really good food. The bar is set higher for alternative approaches – that's the natural conservatism of people at work.

Cars are a great example. Every aspect of electric cars has to be better or at least comparable to conventional ICE (internal combustion engine) cars – anything less and mass adoption is inhibited. We just want faster horses, as Henry Ford knew, until someone shows us the radical new way to travel. Electric cars have to be better horses – that's all.

So, we made the Nemesis with supercar performance. In 2012 we broke the land speed record for an electric vehicle, clocking 151mph in a two-way time trial at Elvington Airfield in North Yorkshire. It was quite a big deal – I did a live radio interview from the site with John Humphrys and we talked about recharging (always the burning question); I told him it took about the same time as it took to have a cup of coffee. That was our sweet spot for motorway charging – about 20 minutes. He thought that was too long. I scoffed (involuntarily) at that comment. It seemed silly to me.

The first 'electricity pumps' we put on the motorway were essentially three-pin plugs – the domestic standard putting out about 3kW. We knew it wasn't good enough and we were honest about that, but if you were an early adopter and had an electric car it was way better than nothing, and we expected the technology to move quickly – it's important not to be limited by what's possible today. Within maybe 18 months we were installing 50kW fast chargers – a huge step up. These could charge a Nissan Leaf in 20 to 30 minutes, the cup-of-coffee-time sweet spot.

We powered the Electric Highway with green electricity – of course. It was an important part of the whole story for us, and important to communicate. Having an electric car was good, but powering it from renewable energy was the endgame to enable emission-free driving.

It was free to use at the start, for mostly practical reasons as the sums involved were very small and use was difficult to meter. This did have a good spin-off effect, PR-wise – it made a great story. Electric cars weren't just emission free, the fuel was free too. It got harder to sustain this as the fast chargers rolled out and use of energy increased massively.

In the summer of 2016, after five years of being free to use, we started 'charging for charging'. It's still surprising to me today just how upset some people got about this and the kinds of arguments they made because they had become used to getting the electricity for free. To them it was their right to have it so and our obligation to make it so. Use of the Highway dropped, which was interesting, suggesting not all use of it was essential.

We juggled with a few different charging approaches in the next couple of years as we tried to balance the needs of different cars and drivers. The 'splash and dash' was an interesting user need and the introduction of the PHEV (plug-in hybrid electric vehicle) had a big impact. These cars didn't really need to plug in on long journeys, that wasn't how they were designed, and they caused a degree of pump rage from EV drivers who really did need to charge and could see pumps blocked by PHEVs. These cars not only didn't really need it, they would occupy a pump and take very little electricity – due to their small batteries. It was preventing our pumps from doing their job. So we introduced a connection charge, a minimum of £3 – to disincentivise pointless plugging in. Mitsubishi, maker of the very popular Outlander, the car causing the problem, waded into the row – we had to gently point out that the Electric Highway wasn't actually designed for PHEV drivers and they didn't really need it. Although we wanted it to be open to all, we had an issue here. And we needed to prioritise.

While our network was free we had some hilarious misuse abuse too. One guy we could see charging multiple times every day, clocking up huge amounts of time and energy plugged in. It turned out he was a taxi driver doing airport shuttle runs with a Chinese car with a big battery. Others told us how they had bought a Nissan Leaf only because our network was free and they could commute every day for nothing; nice for them and we didn't begrudge it, but some didn't take the change too well. Change is like that.

We went from domestic three-pin 3kW to 50kW charging in the first couple of years. That 50kW was a Japanese standard known as CHAdeMO (don't ask). A couple of years later the European standard CCS (I don't even care) appeared – and in the middle we were supporting a niche standard that only Renault seemed to use. It's been a process of Darwinism, of evolution. We can see CCS becoming the single standard for Europe very soon.

Meanwhile new pumps at 150kW are appearing and the CCS standard can support up to 350kW – which is just incredible.

These new high-power pumps can stick 100 miles in your tank in about five minutes – and this is a transformational point. At the same time, 200 to 300 miles is the new normal range for electric cars – up from 80 to 100 back in the day. The point at which the whole cost of ownership (not just fuel) of an electric car is less than that of a petrol or diesel version is one or two years away, according to the industry. Thus electric cars will have moved rapidly, in just a decade, from early adopter tech – expensive with limited performance – to a place where they beat on every measure – the incumbent tech.

In the years we've been pursuing this there have been constant discussions and competing views on what kind of charging was needed where, and electric cars to some have been seen as a bit special – not in a good way, I would say. We've long argued that electric cars need to become analogous to ICE cars – to be seen as simply better versions. And charging behaviour needs to be the same, analogous to filling up with petrol today. A lot of time and money has been spent on creating new ways to top up, but without properly thinking it through, in my view. It's always been clear that bigger ranges and faster charging were the goals of the car makers – and technically feasible.

The new standards of cars and chargers that are here now make that analogous behaviour possible. So, for example, most people will fill up their cars once a week or even once a fortnight. They don't top up every chance they get, as us early adopter EV drivers used to do. At 150kW plus, it becomes possible to see electric cars being used in the same way, and the issues and questions around on-street, lamp-post and car-park charging will fall into the background.

As we launched Zerocarbonista and conceived of the Nemesis in 2008, forerunner of the Electric Highway, we also built 21 new windmills, almost doubling our fleet of green generators, and spent a record amount of our customers' energy bills on windmills – our 'bills into mills' model in action.

It was a good year. It propelled us in a new direction, into new fields of activity.

A few years after we got started with the Electric Highway, we were approached by Tesla. They were coming to Britain with their cars and wanted to build their own chargers for their own customers. It was an egregious approach in my view and very much from the mould of big American tech companies – the walled garden approach.

The problem I have with it is that we have limited grid capacity and parking space – what we have needs to be universally available, not dedicated to customers of individual car companies for marketing advantage.

We discussed ways of cooperating and entered into a partnership discussion, and not for the first time we were asked for commercially sensitive details. Having been bitten more than once before, we insisted on a legal agreement that prevented misuse of the data they were asking for. That proved to be prescient.

Our discussions took place over several months; we had some locations they wanted to be in and we were willing to accommodate some of their pumps. They said they wanted green electricity to power them and we looked at co-branding, maintenance and all sorts of issues, including their launch and the role we might play in it.

Two things were surprising: how flexible they were willing to be and how long it was taking – given their imminent and very public launch date. That last one increasingly looked odd as the clock ticked.

Then we discovered why: it was a sham negotiation. Behind our backs they were agitating with our landlords, urging them to break their contracts with us and blackening our name with the government. They were about to launch a media offensive to bring all of this to a peak when they made a fatal error. They told us about it. Not intentionally, obviously.

They had a new PR guy on their team called Simon, the same name as our guy who led the Electric Highway. So one Sunday in 2014 our Simon received an email intended for their Simon – the classic autofill error.

This email detailed their plans to break the Electric Highway – it was dark, weird to read, hard to believe at first that it wasn't misplaced humour, but we read and re-read it, could see the truth in it and knew why they weren't fussed about concluding discussions with us. They were busy with a different plan.

I felt like we were facing a cowboy-style culture; they'd approached us for something they wanted, offered us baubles for it and when we refused they decided to just take it.

The very next day we sought an urgent High Court injunction – and got it. Tesla were ordered to stop what they were doing. It was a massive embarrassment just ahead of their launch.

It hit the press. I described it as a smash-and-grab attempt, and Musk's reported response was a lie – claiming we had made excessive demands when we had made none. There were a lot of ideas under discussion, all reasonable, and many had come from them.

Later, through our old friend the discovery process, we would learn more of the plotting and manoeuvring that occurred behind our backs. We saw one angry mail from Musk exclaiming to his team, 'it's our Electric Highway not theirs'.

Despite the experience with Thames Water this was an eye-opener to what some people in business are willing to do to get what they want. It showed me a new level of under-handedness and amorality and revealed the corporate culture of Tesla – led from the top.

Eventually the case was resolved out of court, but not before we had our second experience of corporate bugging and not without a price being paid – I'm obliged not to say how much, but it was a shedload.

It was an existential threat, at the time, to the Electric Highway – but when done and dusted was just another battle that we had to fight against corporate wrongdoing. This is how some people do business and how they give it a bad name.

Fast-forward a few more years to today: the Electric Highway is flying. We have 100,000 members and we power over 1.5 million miles of emission-free driving every month. That's more than any other network in Britain, the biggest of which has 5,000 pumps to our 300 – but we deliver more. That's testimony to our founding choice of location.

The Electric Highway was the right thing in the right place, and it's increasingly in the right time. The electric car revolution is well underway, the big car makers are on board, governments around the world are setting dates to ban conventional cars, the tech is ready, price and performance are right – it's ready to go mainstream.

By 2020 we reached a point where we needed to do something we'd not done before: sell one of our ventures, one of the family really. It's not something I've ever wanted to do.

We can see the need for big investment in high-powered charging, and to keep pace with the rapid increase in car numbers on the roads. We always thought this Highway thing could become bigger than Ecotricity and hoped that it would – but it needs a lot more time and money than we can give it. The right thing to do is pass it on. We're still at the bottom of the hockey stick in terms of electric car growth – the pressures we can see now will magnify quickly.

We'd had approaches before but in early 2020 we started a process, and most of the interest came from energy and oil companies – a very good sign, in my view, for the EV revolution.

And as I write this we've had an offer of many tens of millions of pounds, three offers actually, all incredible sums of money. Especially if you bear in mind that we started this with no visibility of a commercial outcome and no concern for one. We did it because we believed it needed doing.

I often think that in business there's room for zen philosophy – if you don't consciously pursue money, it comes. Green energy was the same for us, we didn't start this to make money. Maybe we got lucky in the things we've done, found ourselves ahead of the zeitgeist and maybe that's why they worked. But then again, maybe we helped bring that shift about – and maybe we wouldn't have if we were focused only on money in our decision making. If we lived to eat.

With losses running at about £1 million a year, the value of the Highway is an indicator of where the traditional energy companies think this market is going. The potential they see. That's good news from my perspective. They can see that electric cars are going to take over.

In preparing for the sale we needed to tot up what we spent on the Highway to date – it's about one tenth of the best offer we have – spread over ten years. If we were venture capitalists we'd think that a very good rate of return. We're more like environment capitalists, or maybe we're venture environmentalists, or maybe just environmentalists using business as a tool. Choose your favourite.

The best part of this for me is what it enables us to do next – it's an opportunity to ramp up our work. We'll reinvest this money in the things we believe in, some existing areas of work and some new frontiers.

In ten years' time, you won't be able to buy a new car that's not electric or at least hybrid. I don't think anyone will make conventional cars by then. By 2040 we'll see a complete transformation of the sector, where most of the vehicles on the road will be powered by electricity – just 20 years from now.

Thirty years after we started with the idea to build a car because nobody else was, to kick-start a revolution that few had dreamed of, I believe it will be complete.

CHAPTER 11
ANOTHER WAY

Looking for another way to do things is part of our approach to everything. Not for the sake of it, but because there just often is a better way to do something and, if you arrive without baggage, often enough you can find it.

We had a busy year in 2010, finding new ways to do old things.

We introduced something entirely new to Britain, green gas, and we built Britain's first big solar project (aka Sun Park).

And we cemented our philosophy of Another Way – with a road name – as we entered a new game.

Green gas was significant; it solved a big environmental problem and dramatically changed the outlook. We could see the pathway to replace fossil fuels with green electricity, but as an environmentalist I always thought that when it came to gas we just had to stop using it – had to give it up one day.

That year I discovered that green gas was being made and put into the gas grid in Europe – this was new. We brought some from a sugar beet factory in Holland, it was made from crop waste, and we offered green gas in Britain for the first time.

Green gas itself wasn't new. It was the ability to scrub it up and put it into the gas grid. That was analogous to putting green electricity into the electricity grid – and it was a very exciting possibility. To me anyway …

Green gas is made from organic material, typically food waste or energy crops, broken down in the absence of oxygen in a process known as anaerobic digestion. The small amounts being made in Britain back then were being burned to make electricity in the same way that we had done with landfill or sewage gas over a decade earlier. It's not a good use of gas from an efficiency point of view – half the energy is wasted as unwanted heat. Just as it is with fossil fuels, by the way.

This new ability to scrub this gas and put it into the gas grid was fantastic, but these two main ways of making green gas were problematic; using food waste establishes food waste as a product, making reducing that waste harder (up to 50 per cent of all food produced is wasted), and energy crops have serious drawbacks, involving intensive agriculture and competing for land that food can be grown on.

We looked for another way to make green gas. We wanted to use this new ability to replace fossil fuels in the gas grid, but more sustainably – and we found grass. Just that. It's a brilliant way to make green gas. We did a quick study of Britain and found enough marginal land to grow enough grass to power all 26 million homes in Britain. This was a scalable vision. It had legs.

Having an alternative to fossil gas completed us and made us a whole green energy company with both green gas and green electricity. It also completed our outlook; we had a way to replace fossil fuels in the energy sector – not just electricity but gas too. It's a core part of our manifesto – green electricity from the wind, sun and sea, and green gas from grass. We have the ability to do this, the natural resources and the technology. It's a key part of our pathway to zero carbon emissions. To a Green Britain.

Building our first Sun Park was fun. Solar power was on the verge of a breakthrough and panels had been around on rooftops for a while, but there were no big ground-mounted projects. We built the first at the megawatt scale and added it to an existing Wind Park to create Britain's first hybrid energy park. The wind and sun are complementary energy sources, both daily and seasonally. With wind, you get twice as much energy in the winter as summer; with the sun, it's vice versa. Sharing a grid connection between two complementary energy sources makes good sense because it's more efficient. Our next step will be to add battery storage as part of a more holistic approach – the Smart Grid.

All of this was business as usual for us in our new normal sphere of operations: energy and transport. Then we did something new. We took something on – not really on purpose – and added serendipity to our list of reasons why we've done things.

In the local paper that summer of 2010, I read about the problems faced by Forest Green Rovers (FGR), our local football club – it had relegation and money problems and was on the verge of folding. Someone from the club reached out to me and I went to meet them and watched a game. I thought it lovely; the location, the people, the atmosphere –

everything about it. I'd not experienced football at this level before. It was very much like live theatre. Visceral.

Football hadn't been a big part of my life until then. I was mad for it as a kid, playing as often as I could until probably my early teens and then drifting away. I wasn't a fan of watching it, though I did go to one game in the Netherlands with my uncle, stopping at bars for chips and frothy lager, which I thought was awesome. Probably because I was 11. I went to watch Norwich once with the milkman, as you do. We met up again maybe forty years later, because of FGR. Funny small world.

My son Rui got his name from a football game. A few years before I bumped into FGR, it was England versus Portugal in the 2006 World Cup in Germany. I went there with Kate, on spec. We bought tickets from a dodgy backstreet outfit (doorman wearing a gun), had a fab time (despite the result – Portugal won on penalties) and when we heard the name Rui on the Tannoy (Portugal's legendary midfielder Rui Costa came on as a substitute) we thought it perfect.

I also started playing football again, maybe 15 years ago.

But that's the extent of it, me and football – I never supported a club, just England. And I never had a plan or dream of running a club. It's not something that ever crossed my mind.

The guys at FGR said they needed some cash to get through the summer, about £30,000 I think it was, and then they would be fine. This might be a story as old as football, but this is how it began – the first step on a slippery slope.

The club was in our backyard, a big part of the local community and we were able to help, so I thought we should.

Simple as that. As summer ended the story was changing; the club needed more money and the chairman told me one day that I 'needed to be chairman'. I thought I really didn't. In fact, it felt like the last thing I needed. I had so much on already. But it was quickly clear that the choice was to take responsibility for the club or walk away and see it fold.

So we jumped in – without thinking beyond those immediate circumstances. It was the start of something big, though I didn't know it at the time. Or realise the extent to which football would come to dominate my life; we, my whole family, often wonder now what we used to do on Saturdays.

It was just a rescue mission at the start. Plug the holes and keep this thing running. It quickly evolved as we bumped into issues – things we couldn't be a part of – and we saw opportunity there.

We needed to bring our principles and our way of doing things to the club, there was no choice in that, and we could see that in the process we would in effect be building a green football club. We could also see the opportunity to communicate to an entirely new audience, one relatively untouched by green messaging: football fans. This would most definitely not be preaching to the choir – but that added to the appeal. The more challenging something is, the more worthwhile it is to do.

We reasoned that football fans were passionate people, and if we could reach them with our sustainability messages we could harness some of that passion and point it towards the environment – and make eco fans out of them. And not just in our own club. We thought we might be able to reach the wider world of football and even sport itself.

So we wove sustainability into the DNA of FGR and we created a new kind of football club – one where the environment and football have equal importance – and a new kind of football fan as a consequence. We have fan groups all over the world, in 20 different countries at the last count; some are fans of football, some are fans of the environment, some are both or become both. They've all become fans of FGR for the stance we take on environmental and ethical issues.

It's amazing to me how FGR has resonated with so many people. Perhaps it shows the ability of sport to connect. Perhaps it shows the power of principles, something missing from the world generally and football particularly. Maybe it just shows a latent desire for things to be done differently to the way they are – for greater sustainability. Maybe we are preaching to the choir after all.

A football club is just another kind of organisation, one with a different purpose than we'd come across before. Football has some unique aspects; there were things about football, the way some things were done, that I didn't like. And things we did that were alien to football. There was a bit of culture shock on both sides. We brought a modern, ethical and businesslike approach to the club, along with our sustainability thing – and we've taken some interesting learnings from football. We've carried that with us; football experience informs our decision making in the wider collective – it has relevance. Overall, it's been a cultural exchange.

At the start of this rescue mission it felt like stepping into quicksand. The problems of the club were bigger than

I'd been told, probably bigger than anyone there really knew; information was hard to come by and unlikely to be reliable when it did exist. At every turn we learned something new.

As an organisation the club was dysfunctional, factional and flying blind on the numbers. It was barely surviving on and off the pitch.

On the pitch, back in August 2010 the club had 13 part-time players who never trained on a full-size pitch. A relegation season beckoned. If it happened this year it would be the metaphorical third time of going under. FGR had survived the last two events only because of end-of-season financial problems of rivals, which saw them swap places at the League Annual General Meeting.

Witty fans of FGR (of which there are many) called this the AGM Cup – and FGR had twice won it. Nobody thought there would be a third time.

Over that first year we started to make improvements – added players, began the gradual shift to full-time status, improved training facilities, started looking at nutrition and sports science – and we survived relegation in the last game of the season, but only on goal difference.

We were playing relegation rivals Tamworth and we just needed a draw. They needed to win to stay up. This favoured us, you'd think – but halfway through the second half disaster struck and they scored from long range, like really long range. I stood with our fans behind the goal and saw it in slow motion.

We lost the game but in the dying moments news flashed around our fans' mobiles (I don't have one so experienced the event vicariously) of another relegation battle and of a team that scored once and then again in the last moments – a roar went up, it was enough to save us on goal difference, incredibly. There was a double pitch invasion, both sets of fans celebrating survival. It was pretty awesome.

Off the pitch, FGR's problems were bigger and more difficult to resolve, though simple to summarise: it was making losses. The question was, how big were the losses and where were they occurring?

Standing in the way of an answer was a lack of reliable information and, as we solved this, we pieced the picture together.

There was an agreement with a brewery, for example, a loan tied to exclusive high-priced beer supply and high interest rates; it was suffocating revenue in return for some cash back in the day, long spent. We paid off the loan to free ourselves. For one thing, we wanted to stock local *real* ale.

A bigger problem was matchday receipts: what came in, where from and where it ended up. There was no information. Just a pile of money at the end of every game.

There were lots of volunteers on the gates with cash bags, it looked open to abuse. I asked who the people were and got an angry response from the club secretary not to question the loyalty of these people. I'm the kind of person who questions most things. For me this wasn't a loyalty question or something to be shrouded in emotion. It just looked wrong, inherently problematic.

The turnstiles themselves didn't count, I mean literally – we had no idea how many people came into the ground, let alone what they paid. So one of our first big changes was to install new turnstiles. The first matchday after that, revenues jumped 70 per cent and never went down from there. These new turnstiles were super-modern, with CCTV and voice alerts, and they could do digital ticketing – smartphone tickets. A real step into the twenty-first century.

The ground itself was relatively posh and built to be able to host League football, so when we did eventually make that jump there wasn't that much that we had to do. The club had moved there in 2005 from about 100 yards away; from the Lawn to the New Lawn. It was expected to cost £3 million to build. I'm not sure that it got completely finished, but it had leisure facilities; a dance studio, gym, sauna, hot tub and pub as well as conference and meeting rooms.

It was a good idea but the location was wrong – the facilities were barely used and losing money, draining cash from the club. One of our early breakthroughs was to establish this fact – there was no information on the performance of any of these functions, nobody at the club had any idea. One by one, we established the numbers and saw that each was making losses.

The club had grown over many years, had done really well, climbed the leagues of non-league (always amused by that distinction) and did so as a volunteer-led organisation.

But it had reached the limit of what it could do. The recent move to the new, bigger ground had put the club in a difficult financial position – was basically killing it. The league itself had grown up around FGR, it had become increasingly professional and full-time. And FGR could not sustain itself at that level. It was barely hanging on.

For me, FGR was at a crossroads, an in-between place. It needed to push ahead or drop back. Where it was, was unsustainable.

From the start I'd thought we should aspire to League Two. Why not? How hard could it be? I knew the previous chairman had the same thought; FGR had all the ingredients, the ground was capable of it, we were just one league away. Though it was a big step to take, football wise.

It took two or three years of hard work to put the club on to a solid footing, to create a modern organisation – in that time we finished tenth in the league three seasons running. We'd achieved stability. On and off the pitch.

The eco transformation took place alongside this. We applied our favourite template: energy, transport and food.

Energy was the easiest. We supplied the stadium with wind energy from our windmills. The closest is just up the road, maybe 1 kilometre away, on top of the hill where we built our first mill and where this whole thing started.

At about the same time as we started this adventure, we bumped into Gary Neville, not literally – we reached out after reading about his plans to build an eco home and his interest in the environment. And he responded.

Gary was planning his testimonial game at Old Trafford and was keen to make sure that whatever he did, eco-wise, was robust. He expected to be challenged. We suggested powering the stadium with green electricity for the game, making it carbon-neutral. And that's what we did. The game was in 2012, Manchester United versus Juventus at Old Trafford, and we draped a 40-foot Ecotricity flag down the front of the stadium, had our name in lights on the pitch side boards and at half time we had a penalty shoot-out – FGR versus the MUFC Academy. Unreal.

Amusingly, although we only had three players in the shoot-out, we'd managed to arrive without enough kit and had to raid the club shop.

Coming out of that game, Gary had a bunch of solar panels from a sponsor and gave some to us. We put them on our South Stand roof and they make about 20 per cent of the electricity we use each year.

He also had an idea for a charity dedicated to this space and invited me to found it with him – Sustainability in Sport. I thought it was a great idea, and we put the name on our North Stand. Though we've not done as much with SIS as we would have liked to, it was on the list for a revamp early in 2020 before the virus hit. Several other versions of the same thing have since sprung up. And of course the UN have got involved too.

Transport was fairly straightforward too – we installed electricity pumps as part of our Electric Highway, out the front of the stadium where we built the new ticket office. And we ran a six-month trial with Nissan, giving every player a Leaf to drive in, that was very cool – and totally against the stereotype of football players in gas-guzzling cars. There wasn't much more we could do.

Our ground isn't easy to get to. We run a park-and-ride service, have very limited parking and it's not easy to walk let alone cycle to – being up a very steep hill.

There were no electric coaches in the world then. We thought about making one but didn't get round to it. Electric buses are in the world now (not yet coaches) and as soon as

Pretty much the whole Ecotricity team at the foot of the Ecotech windmill, just after we installed it in 1999. On my left shoulder is Kate, next to her Tim and just behind him Dane.

Getting a mast ready for export in the late 90s.

John Battle, me and my son Sam (left to right) at the launch of the Thames Water joint venture in 1999.

Me, sat in our old Building Society HQ offices in the early 2000s – the same one that hosted the Thames drama.

The Ecotricity team at the Lord Mayor's show in London
in the early 2000's.

Receiving the Queen's Award from the Lord Lieutenant in 2004.

Me, at the EUFA headquarters in 2019.

The Greenbird, built in 2008 and (still) holder of the land speed record for a wind powered car.

As the virus crisis and lockdown began to bite in 2020, we put up a series of adverts, this one by the A40.

The launch event for the Nemesis in London, 2010.

we get the chance, we'll get an electric team coach for away-match travel.

Food was a bigger issue. It started with what *The Sun* called the 'red meat ban' – I loved that; it dramatised the issue and was great publicity for the cause. We started there and within three seasons we were entirely vegan. We took a gradual approach: no red meat, then white meat, fish, cheese and milk.

Food is where we met the most resistance and gained the most infamy. But for me it's a Borg from *Star Trek* thing: 'Resistance is futile.' We were never going to not change this. I would have rather walked away.

For me, going animal free is always about three things: ethics, climate and health. But this was football and on top of these 'reasons to be vegan' (said in the voice of Ian Drury) the burgers being served were grim; they cost pennies because they were made from the parts of an animal nobody else wanted (lips, ears and bums is not an exaggeration). We replaced them with really high-quality plant food. The idea was to make something that was not just animal free but that people would enjoy eating more. The bar was low.

Some fans said we were dictating what they could eat – we disagreed. We told them we were simply setting the menu like every restaurant or food outlet does, we were doing it according to our principles and, by the way, football (at home) is only two hours every fortnight on average. Why come expecting to eat what you normally eat? Why not come and try something different? We went out of our way to put on really good food, handmade, super-tasty – and often the kind you wouldn't expect at football. Our fans did try it and in a very short period of time this was all history – for us anyway. It's still the big thing that all the visiting media want to talk about nearly ten years later.

Away fans like our food too, and fans of other clubs (that we are not playing) who randomly come to our games just to try it and check us out. These other fans lobby their own clubs – asking why they can't have the same. Perfect.

We get cheeky chants from other clubs, which I love – it's part of football. Sometimes it's a bit mindless, witless really, I've walked past away fans, at our stadium and theirs, and been recognised – a shout goes up: 'Meat! Meat! Meat!' Bless 'em if that's all they got.

At the start, stalwarts of the club said we would kill it if we didn't serve meat, nobody would come let alone eat there – it was radical so you can understand the view – but the opposite happened. Crowds are up nearly fourfold now and food sales have outpaced that. And food has put us on the map.

We made quite a few other changes in the first couple of years. We changed the strip (from black and white stripes to green, obviously), the badge (Barcelona rip-off), the food (where to start?). We changed so many things and yet the thing we got the most stick for, ironically, was what we didn't change: the manager. It's one of football's unique aspects, a strength and weakness too: the focus on results and the propensity to change managers frequently, and often as soon as the going gets tough. We've done it differently.

We changed everything around our manager, Dave, reasoning we couldn't judge his performance until we'd done that and given him the tools to do the job, and the time. It was only with three straight tenth finishes that we decided we'd peaked together and needed a change. By then he'd had five years at the club – he was one of the longest-serving managers in English football. He went on to manage Leeds a few years later. I think they gave him six games – this was during the period when Leeds had 14 managers in six years.

In ten years we've appointed two managers. It's one of the ways we operate differently, I believe it's the right way to be and (as ever) that it brings its own rewards. Our reputation attracts better managers than we otherwise might – they know they'll get a fair chance. And we're progressive and ambitious, which helps too.

We did other things. We made our pitch organic, that's a really important issue, taking the chemicals out of farming. We collect water from under the pitch and reuse it – water is a big climate change issue. We have a solar-powered 'mow bot', an autonomous mower that uses GPS technology to cut the grass. We've taken out single-use plastics, achieved zero to landfill, introduced a reverse sugar tax, before removing sugary drinks entirely. All that kind of stuff.

One of the smallest but most resonant things we did was to rename the road the club sits on to 'Another Way', cementing that part of our philosophy, writing it not large, but small – just a road sign at the entrance to the ground, subtle and no less bold or impactful for that.

We've changed the culture, modernised the fabric and outlook of the club; we've grown our audience and changed the demographic, attracting younger fans and families. We started an academy, have an awesome school ambassador scheme which now reaches beyond our county and have a more locally focused Community Trust.

Oh, and last year we did something that hadn't been done in football before – we appointed the first female head of the academy, Hannah. As I write this, we've just announced the beginning of a girls academy to mirror our boys set-up. We'll start at age seven all the way to 18 and nurture local football talent on a gender equal basis – boys and girls.

The stuff we've been doing hasn't gone unnoticed.

A few years ago FIFA, the world governing body of the sport, described us as 'the world's greenest football club'. We were chuffed with that.

And then the UN got in touch.

They were thinking of starting a programme to engage sport in the fight against climate change, had seen what we were doing and it was pretty much what they had in mind. They invited us to go and talk to them and some other sports bodies about the concept and the work we'd done. That was in Bonn in 2017 at another COP – my first since the nineties. This one was COP 23, my first was COP 3 – 20 years had flown by.

We talked about what might be possible, shared our experiences and became one of the founding signatories of the Sport for Climate Action programme. We helped launch that in Poland in 2019. And I've become a UN Climate Champion for that programme, which is pretty special.

It's a long way from the rescue mission for our local non-league football club.

After Bonn the UN invited us to take part in their Climate Neutral Now initiative – this is a three-step programme for organisations to measure their carbon footprint, reduce it as far as possible and offset the part that's left – to achieve neutrality. We already did the first two, of course: we knew our carbon footprint and shrank it every year – it was 200 tonnes when they approached us.

I'm not a fan of carbon offsetting. We'd not done it before for various reasons – mainly because it's not a scalable solution. We can't offset our way to carbon-neutrality, most offsetting schemes take place in countries with very low emissions and between them they might account for 5 per cent of the global total – so even if we took those whole countries neutral this way, it would be nowhere near enough. Also, offsetting is an easy conscience salve for some people and can give a false sense of having taken care of something. On the other hand, the projects that get funded this way help some of the world's poorest people and offsetting can be a useful bridge to somewhere else.

We decided to do it, reckoning the bigger picture benefits made it the right thing to do. Not least helping the UN promote good practice (the measure and reduce carbon part, at least). We offset our 200 tonnes through a UN-certified scheme and became the first sports club in the world to be certified Climate Neutral by the UN – this was in 2018. A few months later, we picked up the Momentum for Change award from the UN – for the stuff we'd done at FGR.

And as I write this FIFA have just named five clubs globally, one from each confederation or area of the sport, as leaders in fan engagement. They named FGR as the top club in Europe. That was unexpected.

Recognition like this lends credibility to our work, that helps, changes the way others might look at what we do.

Media attention helps too – we get a mad amount of that, from all around the world. It's also an important platform for our message; it reaches people.

I reckon being vegan is the biggest single factor, biggest point of interest – even now, years later. It just doesn't get old.

More broadly our story appeals because it's an improbable combination: football and the environment. It's counterintuitive. How can they work together? How can you run a vegan football club? It's actually quite easy – you just have to want to.

We deliver on the pitch too. I've said it before but it's worth repeating: when you create an eco version of anything it has to be good, at least as good as the conventional version. Entertaining and successful football is a key outcome for us and FGR has just had its most successful decade on the pitch in its long history.

In 2017, in the third play-off in a row in the Conference, each time getting closer than the last, in proper steady progress – lost in the semi-finals in 2015, then lost the final in 2016 – we won the final. We got promoted into the Football League proper – beating Tranmere Rovers 3–1 at Wembley.

We made the nine o'clock news that night, not in the sport section – the main news. Chelsea were in the sport section. We were the smallest club to ever be in the Football League and we were a big story. It went round the world and over the next 12 months we clocked over 2 billion impressions in all forms of media – online, TV, print and radio.

It was at Wembley, at the full-time whistle, that commentator Bob Hunt minted his legendary quote live on air when he exclaimed, 'Swindon, Cheltenham, Bristol Rovers, let me tell you this, next season you'll be eating hummus because Forest Green Rovers are in the Football League.'

We built a new kind of football club, created a new kind of football fan, reached a global audience with our message and had some fun doing it. The fun part is important in everything.

And football has become a new frontier for our work; a platform for reaching people and quite a perfect place to demonstrate our philosophy of 'Another Way'.

It's famously a game of two halves though.

Getting into the Football League and turning the club into a modern, effective organisation is only the first part. Our aim is to reach the Championship. And sustain ourselves there – that part is important. Two leagues above where we are now and one below the Premiership – arguably the pinnacle of the sport globally.

That's a very high level of football to be operating at.

It's madly ambitious and at the same time entirely possible. We've scoped it out. We know what we need to do and we can see the raw ingredients are there.

Location is the key. We need to move, we need to be somewhere far more accessible than we are now. Easier to get to, on foot and by bus, and with more parking.

We need a bigger stadium too, but we need a new one anyway. We've done what we can to green up the one we have – ideally we'd start with a blank sheet of paper and build something special. And we need more room than we have, ideally enough space for training facilities.

I started looking for somewhere not long after the rescue mission began. After a two-year search we found only one place that was suitable, but it is perfect. Right on Junction 13 of the M5 on the gateway to Stroud.

Being on Junction 13 (that number again) will put us pretty much in the middle of a county of about 600,000 people with no big football club. We'll be accessible in half an hour from Bristol to the south and not much longer from Birmingham to the north. And of course we will be very visible. It's here that we can grow our audience and seek to establish ourselves as a Championship football club.

There are two pieces of land there. We spent a couple of years negotiating, first for one piece, then for the other, and then realised we needed both. Our thinking had moved on. From a new home for FGR to something much bigger – Eco Park.

Eco Park will be a new home for FGR, but it will also be a 4,000-job green tech business park. The green economy is essential to our future. We need to make space for that. Our green tech business park will encourage and enable firms to set up in this space.

And we've gone further, adding habitat creation to the concept. There are thousands of new trees and kilometres of new hedgerows to be planted but the biggest single element will be the new wetland area, between the canal and the river – an ideal place.

The sum of all this habitat creation is a forecast 16 per cent increase in biodiversity on the site, over and above what's there today. The fact that we can achieve this and build a new stadium and create 4,000 jobs too highlights how bad farming is for nature – that's what the fields are used for today.

Sustainable development is vital; we need to build homes and places for people to work and we need to make room for nature.

With Eco Park we'll get to push the boundaries of sustainable development.

I have no idea where we will get the money from, but I believe we will cross that bridge when we get to it.

The stadium will be a world-class piece of architecture. It's been designed for us by Zaha Hadid's practice. They were the standout winners of the international competition we ran, looking for radically environmental designs. Their proposal is as radical as it is beautiful – an all-wooden football stadium.

Wood is a sustainable material, of course – we can grow it rather than dig it out of the ground. It's the key to a low carbon footprint for our new stadium because 75 per cent of the lifetime carbon footprint of any sports stadium comes from the materials it's made of – not from its running costs in terms of energy. It's embedded carbon and the more usual materials of concrete and steel are the main culprits.

By using wood almost entirely we'll have the lowest carbon footprint sports stadium the world has seen – at least since the Romans invented concrete.

Zaha Hadid Architects told us afterwards that normally our project would have been too small for them but they were attracted by our environmental ambition so they wanted to do this. For me, it's another good example of the good things that happen when you set out to push boundaries and follow principles.

It took five years to get a planning decision for Eco Park. The first decision was a no in July 2019 and a few months later it was a yes. But just after that we had a general election and politics intervened.

We supported Labour, not for the first time, and our local candidate. Jeremy Corbyn held a rally at FGR in the last days of the campaign, that was fun – and we put up posters around town and in the fields at Junction 13. We nailed our colours – it's a democracy right? Well, that it may be, but we got some pushback. During the campaign we had a visit from the police for having Labour banners on our offices, shocking but true. A local Tory councillor boasted that he knew the chief constable and had complained, and he sent two bobbies round. After the election, Stroud had a new Tory MP and she asked Robert Jenrick, the Conservative Secretary of State with responsibility for planning to 'call the decision in' – to look at it with a view to overturning it. He took four months to decide it wasn't a project that fitted the criteria for a call in, during which time we were in limbo. I'm glad he at least reached that decision and we avoided another legal battle – which surely would have followed. It was nakedly political interference. And speaks to the kind of country we have become.

There's a revolution underway in football and we're happy to be a part of that.

There are two ways to bring change to the world. The first is to do it yourself, the second is to be a catalyst – cause others to do it. The change any of us can do ourselves is naturally more limited than the change we can bring about by being catalysts. But one leads to the other. We do the things we believe in, the things we think need doing – and we hope to be a catalyst to influence others.

We explain to our fans not just what we are doing but why, and we hope they take something home with them, that they become open to making changes themselves. We don't preach, don't tell people what to do – we just do the things we believe in. We lead by example.

And we can see that it works – many of our fans have become vegan or vegetarian, some have solar panels, some electric cars. One stopped me at a game this season to tell me he was vegetarian but not vegan yet, has solar panels on his house, was getting an electric car and was thinking about battery storage at home. I was slightly blown away by that.

There are billions of sports fans in the world; if we can make them fans of the environment, what a difference we could make.

CHAPTER 12
GREEN POPULISM?

How we talk about stuff matters. As much as what we do.

I'm a fan of protest and activism, and oddly of populism.

I'm a fan of Greta Thunberg, of Extinction Rebellion and of Sea Shepherd in particular.

Things change when people speak out, when they protest. Activism is a more enduring form of protest, the pursuit of something more persistently. It brings change, sometimes imposes it.

I've done a bit of protesting, stuff that pops up, when I can. Obviously, I'm an activist for the environment. I want to change the world, make it more sustainable and more socially just. I think the two go together, hand in hand. I've lived my life this way, pursuing a low-impact alternative and then using business as a way to do the same – to bring change that way.

Businesses can be activists. There are a few examples out there of companies that pursue outcomes other than money, that speak out on social and environment issues, just not enough … not yet.

Greta has cut through, I think partly because of who she is, her circumstances – and the nature of our media – but also because of the way she communicates. It's from the heart, raw and emotional. She says it how she feels it. She's dogged, single-minded and focused. I like that, all of it.

Extinction Rebellion (XR) have cut through too, drawn all sorts of people on to the streets, many for the first time, and into conflict with authority. Their call to action caught people's attention, as did their method. It's beyond protesting; it's civil disobedience on steroids, maximum disruption by design, strategic, really bold and very effective. It's exciting too. For a while, it felt like they were on the verge of a breakthrough – a breakdown of the status quo seemed imminent. And then it lost a little momentum – but it was the virus wot did it. I hope they return soon.

It's an interesting organisation with founders but not really leaders – a movement that people join and then interpret and do their own thing with. There are now XR groups for business and for wildlife. In this respect it's like the convoy, like any anarchic organisation or movement. I see it as an 'I am Spartacus' thing. People adopt XR, it becomes part of who they are, 'I am XR.'

XR have cut through with their messaging too, they gave us the Climate Crisis and Emergency Declaration.

We declared a climate emergency last summer, the first business in the world to do that, and we've adopted the XR 2025 target to get to zero carbon. We have to be that ambitious. We aim to hit it in 2021.

Sea Shepherd are probably less well known. They use very direct action, putting themselves and their boats in between the whalers and poachers and their prey. Like Greenpeace but more ballsy. They don't witness wildlife atrocities and protest; they intervene, they stop it happening. That's activism, not protest. That's imposing the change we need.

They've been shot at, had boats rammed and sunk, done some sinking themselves, but never harmed people.

And they walk the talk when it comes to food.

So many environmentalists don't. They fail to embrace the one big change we all need to make – giving up meat. The science is clear. The only groups that do get this are typically animal focused – like PETA and Viva! The broader environment groups don't. They have cognitive dissonance when it comes to food.

Not Sea Shepherd – they're vegan pirates. We fly their flag at FGR, and carry their skull and crossbones logo on our shirts – we need more organisations like them in the world. More joined-up thinkers and doers.

It's simple. Eating animals is wrong: it's cruel and unnecessary. It's harming our health and wildlife and the planet. It's inefficient as a way of feeding ourselves, requiring vastly more resources than plant diets do. It has no redeeming features. Environmentalists, of all people, should get this but so many duck it, hiding behind the myth and conceit that they can carry on, in small amounts, as long as it's good quality, or organic or something.

I most recently bumped into this at Womad in 2019, sharing a platform with Gail Bradbrook, one of the founders of XR. We were talking about sustainability stuff with Jon Snow (from Channel 4, not *Game of Thrones*). We got to the topic of food and I was shocked to hear her say she thought we could still eat meat. And so very disappointed; I thought XR were radical and had joined up the dots.

The first time I encountered this was in 1998 at the UN climate talks (aka COP 4) in Buenos Aires. It was the year after Kyoto and the climate change deniers had geared up in response. We infiltrated their organisation. It was made up mostly of oil and car companies and had one of those names that misdirect – making them sound like the good guys. They met first thing in the morning to plan the day ahead, and we slipped in unnoticed wearing ties and shirts, essential businesslike camo. They discussed who would go where to disrupt progress on what – I listened shocked as they mapped out the day. They had their own secretariat, were super-organised, a group within a group and their goal was to slow down and frustrate the talks. Later at dinner, I had vegan pizza (back then it was hard to order, even though it's only pizza with no cheese) and the Greenpeace crew all had steak. Seriously guys?

I don't know how it is now with Greenpeace diet-wise, but I don't see them campaigning to end animal farming. A few years ago they launched a new ship and I saw their promo video. They proudly showed off the contents of their cold store – it was packed with meat. How can you campaign to save sea life while taking life from land animals?

It's a very species-ist approach that identifies some animals as worth saving (the cute, the cuddly, the more intelligent) while others can be abused for food and treated as a commodity. All meat eaters do this.

I've seen it at the UN too – talking about the role of sport in the fight against climate change and about energy, transport and food, and they get it. But lunch was business as usual – so disappointing. Often the reluctance to act is for fear of the reaction. We need organisations to be bold on this topic and fearless about upsetting the crowd – we did it in football, that pretty much means you can do it anywhere.

Everywhere these conversations take place, how we save the world – food is the elephant in the room.

It's like Kryptonite for treehuggers.

For me it's the essential test, because it's a choice, a simple one – and a selfless one – and anybody that doesn't make it isn't real. I have a problem with people that advocate fighting the climate crisis without accepting we have to stop eating animals. That's what I'm trying to say.

I bumped into Sea Shepherd, maybe ten years ago. I read a story in the *Guardian* and it was exciting: this group I'd never heard of were in the South Atlantic Sea to thwart the winter hunt by the Japanese whaling fleet.

They were running out of fuel. I sent an email offering to help; it took a few attempts to get through, but eventually I did – and we sent them the cash to fill up. I loved what they were doing and badly wanted to help. Help save the lives of whales that were being killed. I didn't care if it was for food or research – as the Japanese bogusly claimed. These are beautiful, intelligent, sentient creatures murdered in a most brutal fashion, their kids as well. And here was a small band of people trying to stop that, not by protesting – actually trying to stop that. More often than not they succeeded. It fired me up.

Greta, XR and Sea Shepherd are all activists but I reckon they are also populists. They cut through, get people fired up and get stuff done.

We need more of that. We need to get people fired up about eco issues. Maybe we can learn from the right-wing populists.

People like Johnson, Farage and Trump.

They excite (they revolt too) with simple messaging, stirring fears – without regard for accuracy and with no accountability. They don't care what they say as long as it works. They're masters of the simple slogan repeated ad nauseam. 'Take back control.' 'Get Brexit done.' 'Build a wall.' 'Lock her up.' Stuff like that.

In the same way that tabloid newspapers appeal to the lowest denominators of human nature; so do these populists. They entertain, they don't inform – in fact they misinform – but they do reach people. They cause change – often stupid and self-defeating – and that's testament to their effectiveness. In communications.

When I first heard it said that a lie can travel around the world before the truth gets out of bed, I thought it a decent way to depict something I'd seen myself. Salacious stuff is far more interesting than plain facts – it doesn't have to be true, probably better if it's not. Made up stuff travels further and faster than facts.

I experienced it in wind energy. Windmills are essentially benign, they do an unarguably good job and virtually no harm. The one thing you can say about them is you can see them. They *are* big.

In the very early days of wind energy we talked to local people about climate change and how we needed to make energy without carbon – it was straightforward stuff – the trade-off was something big in the landscape. It was easy in the beginning but it wasn't long before the anti-wind groups got going, spreading an effective mixture of claims – exotic half-truths and falsehoods – stoking fear and envy. And to counter this we had the relatively dull and boring facts.

These guys just made stuff up, they had no accountability. A classic populist trait.

Claims like: windmills interfere with pacemakers, kill thousands of birds a year and use more electricity than they make. That they interfered with TV signals. The most emotive and effective one was that they ruined house prices.

Against that, what we said was dull. They didn't interfere with pacemakers – there was no basis for that claim. They didn't kill birds or ruin TV signals – if properly sited. There was no evidence of an impact on house prices: all the studies showed none. And they made far, far more electricity than they used.

Just countering claims like these gives credence to them; it's human nature to suspect there's fire where there's smoke. Often the result was that people who otherwise had no objections to a local windmill didn't want to take the risk, or became radicalised against this new 'menace' to the countryside and 'our very way of life'.

It was just a windmill. Britain used to have thousands, they arguably powered the first Industrial Revolution. These were modern versions – well sited they were good neighbours, but you could see them. That was all.

The EU was tarnished in the same way with 20 years of denigration in national newspapers – dishonest, exotic, headline-grabbing claims. We reached a point where Europe was a dirty word, associated with bureaucracy and mindless rules and control, by unaccountable people. This was a long-term propaganda campaign that softened us up for Brexit.

In Brexit, there may be no better example of the power of populists and their way of communicating – they packaged it up as an adventure, a boost to the economy, a bid for freedom, taking back control, a return to greatness. It was all very post-truth and it worked. Though for many people it was a protest vote – against the status quo, the impacts of austerity in particular, all of which was blamed on the EU and on foreigners. Problems are always easy to blame on outsiders.

Star of the show was the side of the bus, the £350 million lie. Johnson and Gove insisted it was real. They don't care, they play fast and loose. Nobody holds them to account.

I think we need a regulator for politics, to impose standards of truth and fact on political statements, to require retractions and corrections. We have it in advertising and it's a fairly simple test – you have to have evidence to back any claim you make. Even newspapers have a regulator, though it's an industry-run body and rather lame. Bit like the regulator for the cops.

Brexit had a lot of ingredients, but chief among them for me was communication. Two decades of shifting public opinions with endless attacks, mostly lies, and then the mother of all propaganda campaigns. Epitomised by the £350 million a week stolen from the NHS ... I paraphrase, but only slightly.

Green issues need to be presented with some of that 'panache', that 'devil may care' simplification and fun-loving interpretive licence. Not dishonesty, but relaxing a bit. Poking fun, rounding up, using everyday language and getting people interested – fired up about these issues.

There's no greater risk or threat to any of us than the climate crisis – if there's a legitimate issue to fire people up about, this is it.

How we talk about stuff matters.

In football we've found a way to connect with people, reach an audience and convey a complex and uncomfortable message – but in an accessible way.

At Ecotricity we have a particular way, an ethos, the way we want our people to be. It's about peer-to-peer relationships and conversations – whoever we are talking to, each other, customers, suppliers. Not talking down or talking up – customers aren't always right, nor are we. It's about using everyday language, not jargon – being conversational.

That's how we need to communicate green stuff.

Green stuff (aka sustainability messaging) needs to be accessible. We have to talk about it in everyday terms to show that it's for everyone. We need to make sure that it's inclusive, open to all of us. It's just normal living but with less impact. Burgers, cars and football, what could be more normal than that, and normally quite impactful on the environment – but they don't have to be.

It comes back to this: it's not about giving stuff up – we can still have energy, still travel and still eat – it's just a different and better way to do these things.

We could be green populists, easy enough. To a degree we already are. But we could do more. Not make stuff up, never that. But we can present things differently.

For example, rather than talk about how we need to get to 100 per cent green electricity on the grid to fight climate change and all that good stuff, imagine running a campaign for energy independence instead.

That's what renewable energy can actually give us – energy made here, from our own natural resources, supporting jobs here, keeping billions in our economy. We can end our dependence on foreign energy companies and countries, on global energy markets, denominated in a foreign currency and on price-fixing cartels. Freedom from all of that and from oil wars. We get freedom, jobs and a bigger, stronger economy. It's like Brexit but true. If they can sell that we can sell this.

It's the same thing looked at differently. Communicated differently.

This new way of living that we need has to be presented as an opportunity. That's actually what it is, if we look past the drivers to the outcome.

How we talk about stuff matters.

We don't have to become them, those populists. We don't have to change our identity. Just learn something from them.

And up our game.

CHAPTER 13
MANIFESTO

Modern life is killing us. It should be obvious.

It's driven by the mass burning of fossil fuels, which began with the Industrial Revolution about 150 years ago. And the mass consumption of animals, which began with industrial-scale animal farming about 50 years ago.

These are relatively recent events in human history. Modern problems.

We've reached a place where we consume historically huge amounts of fossil fuels and animals – sometimes we even burn animals to make energy. That's how crazy we've become.

These acts of unhinged consumption are the root of all of our big problems.

The climate crisis, the extinction of wildlife and multiple human health crises, from zoonotic viruses, superbugs and diet-driven chronic illnesses. And the poisonous air we breathe.

Fossil fuels and factory farming cause all of this. That's a fact.[1]

What we need to do about it is obvious.

We need to end fossil fuels. And end factory farming.

To do this we need to change how we power ourselves, how we travel and what we eat.

It's all about energy, transport and food.

In energy we need to replace the fossil fuels we use to power our homes and businesses – we need to make all of our electricity and gas from renewable sources. Green electricity from the wind, sun and sea. Green gas from grass.

In transport we need to replace fossil fuels by electrifying everything: cars, trucks, buses, trains, even ships and planes. We need to power these modes of transport with green electricity.

And in food we need to replace animals with plants.

In all three we need to use less, waste less and source what we do use sustainably.

There are three sectors of society that need to act – government, business and people.

Governments have the big levers: taxes, subsidies and regulations, the tools that create markets. All markets are shaped by these fundamentals. As Thatcher nearly said, 'there is no such thing as a free market'. Taxes and subsidies stimulate, reward and enable the kind of behaviour and economic activity that governments seek.

Regulations set the boundaries: what can, what can't and what must be done.

Business has the role of provider of things – products and services, making available the tools for people to live a zero carbon life. Business is also the provider of jobs and the essential engine of growth for any economy – in this case the green one. Business needs to adapt to create the new industries which will replace the old. And help people adapt.

Henry Ford knew it; people want what they are comfortable with, what they know. But businesses can shift the paradigm and introduce the things that nobody wants yet. The new things.

Henry Ford did it. We did it with green energy.

People have the ultimate responsibility; consumption is the root cause of carbon emissions and our associated problems. As people we are responsible for these crises, they're driven by the things we spend money on every day – 80 per cent of our own carbon footprints are within our control this way. We have to demand change and make change – in our own lives. Companies and governments will respond to that.

Government sets the framework, business adapts, and people respond.

But not necessarily in that order.

HOW TO GO ABOUT IT

In energy it's about the electricity and gas we use in our homes and businesses.

Electricity is the most straightforward. We can make all of the electricity we need using the wind, the sun and the sea. We already have over 30 per cent of our electricity[2] made this way – we just need to close the gap to 100 per cent.

The technology is reliable, affordable and mass-produced. We have the natural resources – enough wind and sun to power our country more than ten times over. We have the industry. We could reach 100 per cent green electricity in ten years. It's the most advanced sector and easiest for us to complete the transformation.

One hundred per cent green electricity on the grid is a technical challenge but we know how to solve it. The Smart Grid concept: the real-time balancing of generation using intelligent demand, buffered by grid- and home-scale battery storage. This is happening now.

In the Smart Grid, homes and businesses will be interdependent with the grid, not dependent on it; giving and taking according to different circumstances. Local grids will be interdependent with each other, forming a new dynamic national network – no longer top down and centralised but something else altogether. Technology will enable this through machine learning and AI.

Interconnectors with other countries complete the puzzle. We have them now, and they can be used to balance the availability of renewable energy as the weather moves in broad fronts.

Hydrogen is being pushed as a way to store excess electricity instead of batteries as part of the Smart Grid. But it makes little sense to me; the process of using electricity to make hydrogen and then hydrogen to make electricity (power to gas to power) is as inefficient as it is long-winded to describe, with a round-trip efficiency of less than 50 per cent. By contrast, battery storage is around 90 per cent and growing – and it's here now; we don't need to build a new industry.

Hydrogen is cool. The idea we can make it just from water makes it so, and it's clean in use. To a degree it's a solution looking for a problem. Energy storage is not the right problem; we have better ways to solve that and better ways to use hydrogen.

Gas looks like a harder problem to solve. At least according to conventional wisdom which frames this as the 'de-carbonisation of heat challenge' with the focus on how we switch from using gas for heat to using electricity instead.

But conventional wisdom, one of my favourite oxymorons, is mistaken. We don't need to stop using gas for heating: we can make green gas. The technology and natural resources exist to do this.

We can make green gas and deliver it through the gas grid. Use the infrastructure that we already have and the tens of millions of existing gas appliances. It's by far the better way.

In the process we can create a new industry.

Ecotricity produced a study a few years ago that showed we have enough spare land to grow enough grass to power all 26 million homes in Britain. In the process creating 75,000 jobs in the rural economy and turning vast areas of land into wildlife habits. Green gas is thus not just part of the answer in the energy sector, it also offers a transition for farming, as we change our diets.[3]

Businesses in Britain also use gas, about two-thirds as much gas as homes do,[4] so we will need more land for this, but the study we did for homes was for existing land not in use for food production. If we factor in the freeing up of farmland from a diet change, we free up 50 per cent of Britain's total landmass and we have far more than we need.[5]

It's an interesting relationship. Changing our diets frees up land we can use to make gas which creates jobs in the rural economy and a transition pathway for farmers. We'll also create natural fertilisers for plant farming – it's a by-product of green gas. We need to replace artificial fertilisers, they're made from fossil fuels.

It's good economics too.

We burn £9 billion worth of fossil gas per year in Britain;[6] increasingly that money leaves our economy. We produce less than 50 per cent of the gas we need now,[7] as North Sea production and reserves shrink. That money doesn't need to leave our economy; we can spend all that money on gas made here.

It's an incredible opportunity to solve a big climate issue, create an entire new industry and economic activity. And proper sustainable gas – carbon-neutral and renewable.

Hydrogen has a role here. We can make it by splitting water with electricity and put it into the grid as green gas.

This process has an efficiency of about 75 per cent – half the losses of using hydrogen to store electricity, because the hydrogen is used directly for heat. This is just 'power to gas'. Half the steps, half the losses.

It's not a new thing. Hydrogen has been in the grid before – and all new gas appliances in Britain since 1996 are capable of operating with a 23 per cent hydrogen mix. So we're ready to go, grid and appliance wise.

Hydrogen can contribute roughly 20 per cent of our gas needs.[8] It's a decent chunk and there's a neat way to make it.

As we push to 100 per cent green electricity on the grid we inevitably have to oversize the generation fleet; we will create times of surplus, in order to minimise times of shortage – that surplus of green electricity could be used effectively to make green gas by splitting water into hydrogen. It's a neat combination. And gas is relatively easy to store, unlike electricity.

And the seasonal nature of wind means the big surplus from that tech will be in winter – when we need most gas. That's a good fit.

In energy, we have all the ingredients. The natural resources, the technology, the infrastructure (gas and power grids) and an industry ready and able to scale. We can replace fossil fuels, and fossil fuel jobs and the fossil fuel industry.

It's a theme of the Green Industrial Revolution – moving from the old way of doing things to the new doesn't destroy jobs and industry per se. It replaces what we have with what we need.

Making our own energy is not the only thing we need to do. We need to save it too.

The cheapest energy we can make is the energy we don't use, through avoided consumption. Energy efficiency should feature prominently in our plans. Home insulation is a relatively inexpensive way to cut carbon. And it helps keep future energy bills lower.

To achieve this transformation in energy we need big but simple changes from the government.

Everything the government does today favours fossil fuels. We need to shift that bias towards renewable energy and keep shifting – ultimately leaving no role for fossil fuels at all.

Government has to plan for the end of fossil fuels and make it so.

It can do this with the three big levers: taxes, subsidies and regulations.

Taxes and subsidies are really two sides of the same coin – a tax break is a subsidy, they both provide financial support and incentive from different sides of the equation, but it amounts to the same thing. In Britain today we spend 25 per cent more supporting the fossil fuel industry than we do the renewables industry (£10 billion versus £8 billion). Globally the figure is 100 per cent – and some of that support comes from Britain.[9]

We need to rapidly transition away from fossil support towards renewable support and ultimately to zero fossil support. The net cost of this is nothing; it's a transfer of spending from the bad stuff to the good stuff. If we shift £2 billion a year from fossils to renewables, at the end of the first year they would be reversed in position (£8 billion versus £10 billion). Within five years we would be spending no money on fossil fuels – that's long enough for a transition, and long enough to keep chucking vast sums into this dirty old industry.

It can't make sense to keep spending money on fossil fuels. Government has to grasp this.

Green energy bizarrely pays a carbon tax, even though it produces none. Large energy users are exempt from the same tax, even though they use fossil fuels – producing carbon. Anomalies like this have to go first.

Regulations also need to change, like the planning system which currently favours fossil fuels, and actually prioritises them despite their climate impact – as a string of recent planning decisions has confirmed. We've launched a legal challenge to try and change this. Ideally we'd have a government that didn't need challenging through the courts to do something as simple as matching (climate crisis) words with deeds.

Current planning rules also hold back renewables, there's a systemic bias against them. It's crazy really.

We need to ban all new fossil-fuelled projects in the energy sector, right now, build no more – and of course ban fracking. Green projects should have the prioritisation currently enjoyed by fossils – and more, they should be fast-tracked through planning.

People have a role too, there's stuff we can do at home like use less energy and make our own.

For that we need government too: currently there's 20 per cent VAT on solar panels for home use, but 5 per cent for use of coal. Another anomaly that needs correcting.

Green energy and energy-efficiency equipment should be zero rated for VAT at least – to encourage and enable the tackling of these issues at the point of consumption – in our homes.

Reshaping the market by changing taxes, subsidies and regulations will enable us to move rapidly to end fossil fuel use in this sector. In fact, it's all we need.

Through these steps alone we can tackle the issue upstream; at the production end we can make the grid entirely green.

Stuff we can do at home, downstream, augments this and is a vital part of the building out the Smart Grid.

In transport we just need to electrify everything.

Cars, trucks, buses, trains, planes, you name it … even ships. And it's possible.

For ships wind power is making a comeback. Not just with modern versions of sails, but blades of the type we see on modern windmills – both are being used to augment propulsion. It's a great piece of 'back to the future', which can help clean up shipping.

Electric cars are here – this change is well underway. Car makers are planning for the end of the internal combustion engine. Within ten years the only new cars available to buy will be electric.

Electric buses exist, they're on the road in small numbers in Britain, but in large numbers (hundreds of thousands) in China. They make great sense in cities and towns from a noise and pollution point of view. Even if the climate crisis didn't exist we should be doing this.

Electric trucks are in R&D, but they're surely coming.

The bigger the platform – buses and trucks versus cars – the easier to electrify, the easier to carry the batteries required.

Electric trains have been possible for a long time, of course, but use overhead power lines which are expensive to install. Recent advances in cost and performance of batteries (driven by the car industry) opens up a new possibility: electric trains running on conventional tracks. Instead of carrying diesel with them they can carry batteries. This makes electrification of all train lines possible.

Electric planes are more of a challenge. Perhaps surprisingly there are electric planes in the skies now, small ones and in small numbers. But in ten years the major manufacturers, Boeing and Airbus, both expect to have short-haul electric planes in production.

And the carriers are engaged – EasyJet is part of a programme to develop 500-mile range, 186-seater electric planes for use by 2030.

Long-haul flights are a bigger challenge, but synthetic jet fuel is possible: we can make it from atmospheric carbon. It's expensive but properly carbon-neutral and the only way that long-haul flying can be, albeit a big technological breakthrough, though that may yet come.

This new jet fuel will become less expensive as the industry required to produce it scales up and technology improves: demand for it will make this happen. We need to start using it now.

Long-haul flights will still be possible, we'll value them more and use them less, if we price more realistically – at the price of zero carbon damage.

Does hydrogen have a role in transport, delivering electricity using fuel cells instead of batteries? I don't think so. Other than in niche applications.

Hydrogen used for transport suffers the same fundamental problem as hydrogen used for electricity storage; it's actually the same thing. The process of 'power to gas to power' results in a round-trip efficiency that's roughly half that of a battery-powered vehicle – so we need twice as much green electricity to travel using hydrogen as with batteries.

Environmentally that's a non-starter. Why make the job twice as hard as it needs to be?

There's plenty of lobbying for hydrogen. It suits the current business infrastructure of the big oil companies – refineries, tankers and forecourts. But it doesn't make sense. We have a far better way of delivering green electricity to our wheels.

Electrifying transport creates a crossover opportunity, from the transport to the energy sector. Today the combined power output of all the cars on the roads of Britain is bigger than that of all our power stations. With an electric fleet this size we would have a dispersed battery storage capacity capable of playing a significant role in the balancing of energy supply – the Smart Grid. The jargon for it is V2G – Vehicle to Grid – it's about using vehicles to give power to the grid as well as take from it. And though it's often a bit hyped by industry interests – it has potential.

We can electrify all forms of transport, except planes for long-haul flights – and for those we can use genuinely carbon-neutral fuel, unless and until a breakthrough comes.

We can replace fossil fuels in the transport sector with green electricity. It's a bigger job than transforming the energy sector, multifaceted and less advanced – but it's entirely doable. And no less important.

We just have to shift ourselves from the horses we have to the horses we need.

We should rethink cities and towns, deprioritise the car and reprioritise pedestrians and cyclists – let's reclaim the streets.

And rethink work itself. Blended working, from home and office, could be one of the big takeaways from the virus crisis – reducing travel significantly.

Government has the same role here as in energy, to tip the economic balance, and shape the market in favour of electrified transport and synthetic jet fuel. Using taxes, subsidies and regulation.

Fuel duty is an example – it's a tax on pollution and a key tool in the transition. Road fuel duty should be unfrozen and ratcheted steadily up, with the revenue spent supporting electric vehicle adoption.

And fuel duty should be applied to aviation fuel: it makes no sense to continue to exempt it. The economic arguments for supporting the aviation industry don't stack up.

We should end duty-free shopping at airports. Or extend it to cover bus and train use and level the playing field that way. I'm kidding – it should stop, it makes no sense to reward flying, the most polluting of all forms of travel.

Government should electrify the railways. We need to end airport expansion. We can use what we have more wisely, more fairly.

It's a myth that a booming aviation sector is essential to economic growth. And given that just 1 per cent of Britons take 20 per cent of all flights and 10 per cent take over 50 per cent, it's not about enabling holidays now: it's a regulated industry so it's in their control.[10] The technology exists and the cost is far lower than the traditional approach of overhead lines – it's a big, affordable, quick win. Way cheaper than HS2, the £100 billion high-speed rail project that will wreak huge environmental damage.

Low-emission zones should be the norm, these will help support electric modes of transport and haulage.

Inner-city air quality is a crime, literally: it's at illegal levels. Electric road transport can fix that. Taxing pollution is taxing crime.

There's a role for government in electric vehicle charging infrastructure, though not by funding it. We need to accommodate the charging of over 30 million electric vehicles, for that we need strategic grid reinforcement and investment. The private sector is not suited to the job. The local and national grid companies are best placed: they should build it and pay for it, and recoup the cost over the next 20 years through use of system charges – the cost they levy for the use of their networks. Electric vehicles will bring increased network use so it makes sense to deal with it this way.

They are regulated monopolies – we can regulate them to get the outcome that we need. A grid fit for the job – for tens of millions of electric vehicles. It's a big job.

In food we just need to replace animals in our diets with plants.

We've no real need for technology in this sector. Plants are simpler, safer foods to handle and process (if you process them) and to eat.

What we need here is behaviour change. The shift has begun, we need to push it.

We need more available, better-priced and better tasting plant food to facilitate this change. All of that is underway because business is responding to demand from people.

We need to pump up that demand with communications on the issues of health, cruelty and need. We need to make people aware of what they are eating, how it's made and what it's doing to them.

All change starts with communication, about the problems and about the answers.

Health is a key issue. People are already choosing to eat less meat and dairy for health reasons,[11] rather than the more altruistic ones, like climate and animal rights. That's a signpost for how to cut through.

Cruelty matters too. People are basically decent and care about how animals are treated; we need to surface the reality, the unpalatable truth about how meat and dairy are produced. When people learn of this, change becomes easier.

We experienced this at FGR, with cow's milk. When we took it off the menu some of our fans wanted to know why. I asked them if they knew how milk was produced; they didn't, so I told them about it. The endless cycle of pregnancy and separation of mother and calf at birth, and the killing of the newborn but unwanted male calves – all so humans can have that mother's milk. It's cruel and heartless. But it's not how the milk industry markets itself; people think cow's milk is a harmless product, some kind of natural surplus. Not many people will insist on it when they know how it is produced and when oat milk is such a good alternative.

Add this to the negative health impacts of animal products, like milk, and it's a powerful combo.

Climate change is just the icing on the cake.

Need is an important issue to deal with too – the pervasive myth that we need to eat animals. Science says otherwise, we need to share that.

Vitamin B12 is a good example, it's a myth that we need to eat animals to get enough B12 in our diets. It's maybe the most persuasive and hardest to counter; B12 is relatively hard to find in all foods, though it's worth saying that vegans tend to be less deficient in it than the general population.

But 90 per cent of all the B12 we produce as food supplements is fed to factory-farmed animals (95 per cent of all meat) because their lives are so unnatural. They can't get it any other way. They would normally get it from contact with bacteria in the soil, when grazing, but of course they never get to go outside, except for the trip to the slaughterhouse.

They are deficient in B12 and they need supplements – you couldn't make it up. We don't need to eat these animals to get B12 – we can just eat the supplements that we feed to them instead. How crazy is our food.

There are other issues that we need to look at.

The amount of food we import is generally reckoned to be 50 per cent, which sounds high. But this figure doesn't include imported ingredients that are processed here. The real figure, if we include imported ingredients, is 80 per cent.[12] That's too high. It's a dependency and makes us vulnerable to shocks in the global food system.

I don't think we can realistically aim or need to be food independent but we should aim to improve on this figure, for reasons of resilience not least. There's economic benefit too, in taking more responsibility for our own food production; we spend £40 billion a year on food imports.[13]

We don't need to worry about food miles though, perhaps counterintuitively, and it's a good example of where the media misdirects with its own approach. What we eat is more important than where it comes from. Way less than 1 per cent of the carbon impact of food is from food miles. It's not something to stress over.

Food waste is a problem; up to 50 per cent of all food produced is estimated to be wasted.[14] It's mad that we make twice as much food as we eat.

We can replace animals with plants easily enough. It's not a question of technology, like in energy and transport – plants are simple, it's a back-to-the-future move. It's all about behaviour change and how we encourage more of what's already happening.

Government gets the same job here: reshape the market to make the production and consumption of the bad stuff – animals – less economic than the good stuff – plants. It is the natural order of things, after all. Taxes, subsidies and regulations are the keys.

The cow tax that we suggested five years ago in our vision of what 2030 could look like, looks less radical now. We should have one – like with fuel duty, call it meat duty. It makes sense. We have to tax impact.

Meat has zero VAT but nuts are charged at 20 per cent. Let's start with imbalances like this.

Let's point the £3.5 billion we spend subsidising farming in the right direction – transition it to plants.

We need to make animal farming more expensive through regulations too, insisting on actual animal welfare and humane slaughter – not just in words but in deed. What's done today to animals in factory farming in pursuit of money over everything is abhorrent.

We need to end factory farming. We can transition our way there using economic levers.

We actually need to emancipate animals. I know that's a big ask right now, but one day it won't look so.

Government needs to tackle demand for animal products too. It's based on habit and false marketing. The idea that we need animal products and that they are good for us. The science says otherwise.

Government advice has fallen behind; there's an unwillingness to go against the farming and big food lobbies. The science is clear though – eating animals is bad for our health and we don't need animals for complete nutrition. We need a public health campaign to make this clear. Green populism might have a role here, to help us cut through. It's one of the key ways to persuade people to change what they eat. It's in their own interests.

This is a situation analogous to that with smoking where for years the industry denied a link to bad health – even sold smoking as a healthy habit (as with meat and dairy) – and governments were slow to act, but when they did it was with a series of incremental moves, increasing taxes to fund the health cost, health warnings of increasing severity, an advertising ban and ultimately brand-free packaging with hideous pictures of health impact. We have a blueprint, this is the way to go.

We should highlight the increased risk of cancer and heart disease, for example, on product packaging. Maybe add some pictures from factory farms too – to show the genuine provenance of what's in the packet. We need some science and some honesty in food. And some boldness.

Government also needs to regulate the processed food industry; the three main (overloaded) ingredients of all processed food are salt, fat and sugar. It's a crime against our health and our taste buds, which are overwhelmed, making ordinary food taste tasteless, which then perpetuates the need for processed food.

As with all parts of the Green Industrial Revolution, we need a transition. Farmers can diversify, not just into plants – green gas and wildlife habitats are a cross sector and big opportunity for that. Businesses can adapt and for the end user, we the people, plant food is super-tasty, clean and healthy. Everybody wins.

We need a new Industrial Revolution. And a new way to live.

It's not so grand or complex as it sounds. We need to change two things – how we power ourselves and what we eat. Everything else will flow from that.

Food is actually the key issue. The food industry is one of the biggest drivers of the climate crisis but it's also driving wildlife extinction and multiple health crises.

Changing what we eat unwinds these issues and unlocks other opportunities; vast wildlife areas acting also as carbon sinks, the ability to make the gas we need from grass – and a just transition for farming. It's a cascade effect.

Imagine rewilding half the landmass of our country.

Our food choice can do this.

It can also tackle the huge health crisis that our diets have created. All of the major chronic diseases that affect us in later life are linked to a diet of animal products. They don't just kill, they make life miserable. Chronic diseases are not cured; they are managed to the point of death.

Meat is not murder. It's murder suicide.

Meanwhile, the energy industry isn't just driving climate change and air pollution. It drives inequality and injustice.

Fossil fuels cause conflict and wars because they don't occur equally around the world, we compete for them commercially and militarily. They're finite: it's only a matter of when they run out. The price of fossil fuels is controlled by a global market – manipulated is a fair description.

Renewable energy by contrast is universally available, it occurs in all parts of the world. It won't ever run out, not while our sun lasts, so forever in this case means a few billion years.

It is in all respects abundant – an endless supply, everywhere. We don't have to compete or fight for it, and we don't need a global market setting the price of it.

Renewable energy can democratise energy.

You may have heard the old maxim, 'It's the economy, stupid.' Bill Clinton used it in the early nineties.

The way I see it is: 'It's the stupid economy.'

The way we power ourselves makes little economic sense.

We spend £50 billion a year bringing fossil fuels to Britain just so we can burn them.[15]

It's not just a big cost – it's an uncertain one.

The price of fossil fuels is set by international markets, influenced by economic outlook, sentiment and by supply and demand, while supply is manipulated, quite openly – by the producers. These factors have led to the price of oil fluctuating between $20 and $160 per barrel over the last 70 years.

This fluctuation does not represent the changing cost of extraction – it's artificial. This market is Frankenstein's monster, a product of free-market dogma and anything-goes capitalism – with a bit of geopolitics thrown in. It dominates our world.

The £1 billion a week we currently spend importing fossils could easily be £3 billion based on historic market prices. And more when the North Sea is emptied.[16]

Because oil is denominated in dollars we have the exchange rate fluctuation to contend with as well. More uncertainty.

Price and exchange rate fluctuations bring great unpredictability and jeopardy to our economy – it's way beyond our control. We're a price taker not a price maker – to use Brexit terms.

We spend another £10 billion a year on subsidies for fossil fuels.[17] To make them cheaper to burn. That makes good sense – obviously (not).

We can invest instead in the infrastructure to harness our own sources of green energy – it has zero fuel cost and zero price fluctuation and we can pay ourselves for it. We can free ourselves from this crazy market that dictates so much.

In the process we can create hundreds of thousands of sustainable jobs in new industries and a more stable and sustainable economy. This is what energy independence looks like.

Our diets are a 'stupid economy' issue too.

It's inefficient to feed ourselves with animal products.

We can feed up to ten vegans or one meat eater with the same amount of plant food – that's how it works. Right now, half of Europe's cereal production and 98 per cent of the world's soya is fed to animals to achieve incredible reductions in both calorific and protein value.

It's bonkers in economic terms to reduce the value of the food we grow (plants) by passing it through animal bodies (polluting it). If we were madly rich and there was no climate or wildlife impact, or animal rights issues, or human health, maybe it would be a reasonable choice – but none of these conditions apply.

This inherent inefficiency is the reason why a plant diet would free up three-quarters of Britain's farmland. Half the landmass of our country.

We spend over £3 billion a year in Britain on subsidies to make this food artificially cheap.[18]

Our diets don't make economic sense. We're making food far more expensive than it needs to be and subsidising it to try and offset that inherent extra cost, all while millions of Britons live in food poverty. And we spend tens of billions in health costs on diet-driven illness.

Add it all up and it really is pretty stupid given it's a choice.

Changing our approach to energy, transport and food is not just about climate change, wildlife extinction and human health – it's about economics too.

Green energy could be at the heart of a new economic order.

The cynic might suggest that we don't pursue green energy over fossils precisely because of these attributes; it's not only found in certain parts of the world, it can't be controlled by half-a-dozen large companies and countries, by any cartel – there is no market required, no price that fluctuates with supply and demand. We can supply all demand. It's a decentralised, universally available, endless source. We can't use it up.

Do vested interests hold us back?

We do need to leave behind vast conventional industries, markets and energy reserves, and upset the economic and geopolitical pecking order – that is a problem, there is resistance to that.

A world powered by renewable energy would also undermine the dollar as the go-to international currency – oil markets denominated this way create fundamental demand for that currency. Global renewable energy use will undermine the global political order. In a good way.

Green energy has a lot to offer. It's nothing less than a revolution. Resistance is to be expected. We can be Borg-like about that.

'Business as unusual.' I first heard this term coined by Anita Roddick, founder of the Body Shop. It's what we need.

Business has a vital role to play – it has unique abilities. But we need to repurpose it as well as capitalism: end the pursuit of money above all else and require businesses to deliver social and environmental outcomes – not just lip service corporate social responsibility type stuff – but actual outcomes, measured and reported just like the conventional bottom line.

This is our society, we get to set the rules – and the rules for being able to run a business should include an obligation to deliver more than money to shareholders.

Government has a role here as a regulator of all things, but also through using the tax system.

Corporation tax in Britain is too low; at 18 per cent it's one of the lowest in the world. It's lower than the income tax we pay as individuals, which is wrong. But it's also uniform, one size fits all.

We should have a higher starting rate, I suggest 30 per cent with incrementally lower bands for companies that achieve environmental and social outcomes. Maybe down to 20 per cent for those that achieve carbon-neutrality. That's where we need to be as a country. It makes sense to incentivise companies to get there.

We could make tangible environmental and social outcomes tax deductible, in effect.

This incentivises good behaviour and enables it to be paid for – it creates the budgets for investment, for better outcomes.

The case is often made that higher tax is a disincentive to businesses or entrepreneurs – and that it reduces a business's ability to bear overheads or to grow – it's manifestly false. Business tax was 26 per cent not many years ago, and slashing it did not unleash a wave of growth. It unleashed greater corporate and investor profits. That's all.

Tax cannot be a disincentive to running a business any more than it is a disincentive to having a job. Business tax doesn't need to be lower than the rate of personal tax to encourage business owners to 'get out of bed' so to speak. That's a myth.

Ecotricity is a mission-led, not-for-dividend company. We reinvest the money that we make into the things we believe in. We know that businesses can operate in this way – the question is should we continue to let them operate any other way.

Pursuit of money above all else leads to poor decisions and ultimately to poor environmental and social outcomes. Business got us where we are today, in many senses, but in terms of the multiple crises we face – absolutely so.

We need to repurpose it and use it to get back to a better place.

Maybe the right parallel for these times is to say we need to be like a virus to business: we need to infect it, take it over and use it to our own ends.

It becomes a virtuous circle as we make this transition away from a fossil fuel economy, underpinned by capitalism of the money '*über alles*' kind, and towards renewable energy and a new kind of business model. We can tackle poverty and injustice at the same time as the climate crisis. And make a better system than the one we have.

We need a government that gets it, though, because we can't do this unless the rules of the game are changed. We need taxes, subsidies and regulations pointing Another Way.

I think politics is the next frontier – where we most need change and where most impact can be had. I may go there.

It's all waiting to be done; dump the fossils, save the animals, save the climate and save ourselves. Build a sustainable economy, end food and fuel poverty and global conflict – mostly.

Ecotopia awaits.

EPILOGUE

Often the things we need to do look difficult or impossible, but new stuff is like that. Before you know it the impossible becomes the norm.

I want to leave you with this.

Some years ago, I was thinking about the concept of geoengineering as a way to extract carbon from the atmosphere. That led me to think about how to store that carbon, and to the simple thought that the most permanent, enduring form of carbon – the toughest of all – is a diamond.

I wondered if it might be possible to take carbon from the atmosphere and turn it into diamonds. I loved the idea, and not just as an environmentalist; it's radical and evocative – it's modern-day alchemy. So we pursued it.

Five years later we've done it. We're making diamonds from atmospheric carbon.

Diamonds literally from the sky.

The few people I've told about this have all looked at me like I must be joking or might be slightly crazy. And fair enough, I feel crazy saying it. As an idea it's out there – more so than the idea of green energy back in the day.

And maybe it was more of a mission impossible than that first windmill.

But we've made it real, and I hope it will become the new normal.

We're using green technology to tackle the climate crisis and challenge an entire industry, an old way of doing things that causes much destruction, pollution – and social harm. As the old ones tend to.

It's a great example of how we can live this new life, without giving stuff up, still having fun – in this case, still having bling. Climate Bling if you like.

Our process uses only the wind, sun and rain – our by-product is cleaner air, since we strip the carbon from it. Our product is anatomically perfect diamonds. Made without pollution, without fuelling conflict, without abusing people.

We're calling them Sky Diamonds.

As I write this it's still a secret – I don't know if this book will hit the world first or if Sky Diamonds will. But I wanted to share it here.

This is green technology as it needs to be – sustainable, ethical and fun.

Our next campaign will be to end diamond mining.

We have Another Way for that too …

RESOURCES

CHAPTER 1

1 https://www.theguardian.com/commentisfree/2020/jun/15/obesity-is-a-major-risk-factor-for-dying-of-covid-19-we-need-to-take-it-more-seriously
2 https://www.medrxiv.org/content/10.1101/2020.04.15.20065995v2
3 https://uk.reuters.com/article/uk-health-coronavirus-britain-business-s/uk-unveils-330-billion-lifeline-for-firms-hit-by-coronavirus-idUKKBN2140V2

CHAPTER 10

1 https://assets.publishing.service.gov.uk/government/uploads/system/uploads/attachment_data/file/733109/nts0308.ods&sa=D&ust=1598361648683000&usg=AFQjCNFMlaZuT5HhTQBWHk0omxICN1XQxQ

CHAPTER 13

1 https://www.peta.org/features/meat-climate-change/
2 https://assets.publishing.service.gov.uk/government/uploads/system/uploads/attachment_data/file/877047/Press_Notice_March_2020.pdf

3 https://www.ecotricity.co.uk/news/news-archive/2016/ecotricity-unveils-plan-for-britain-to-make-its-own-gas-from-grass
4 https://assets.publishing.service.gov.uk/government/uploads/system/uploads/attachment_data/file/904794/DUKES_2020_Chapter_4.pdf
5 https://science.sciencemag.org/content/360/6392/987
6 https://assets.publishing.service.gov.uk/government/uploads/system/uploads/attachment_data/file/820685/Chapter_4.pdf
7 Ibid.
8 https://www.citizensadvice.org.uk/Global/CitizensAdvice/Energy/Citizens%20Advice%20-%20Hydrogen%20for%20Homes%20-%20Questions%20about%20how%20hydrogen%20might%20work%20for%20homes%20in%20Great%20Britain.pdf
9 https://assets.publishing.service.gov.uk/government/uploads/system/uploads/attachment_data/file/857027/UK_Energy_in_Brief_2019.pdf
10 https://www.theguardian.com/environment/2019/sep/25/1-of-english-residents-take-one-fifth-of-overseas-flights-survey-shows
11 https://www.ahajournals.org/doi/10.1161/JAHA.119.012865
12 https://www.businessinsider.com/no-deal-brexit-percentage-british-food-imported-shortages-2019-1?r=US&IR=T
13 http://www.wrap.org.uk/content/quantification-food-surplus-waste-and-related-materials-supply-chain

14 https://www.statista.com/statistics/281818/largest-import-commodities-of-the-united-kingdom-uk/

15 Ibid.

16 Ibid.

17 https://news.sky.com/story/farmers-to-be-paid-to-protect-the-environment-and-improve-animal-welfare-11909574

INDEX

DV indicates Dale Vince.

ACKNOWLEDGEMENTS

I want to thank John Robb for helping me see certain aspects of this story and make it happen. I needed that kind of input.

Will Guyatt because he said I should (and he did help).

My other half, Kate, because she doesn't get much of a mention but she is important.

My youngest son Rui (12 going on 20) – in case I ever needed grounding I have him telling me writing a book about your own life is arrogant…and I know what he means.

All family in Stroud, all part of this in one way or another.

And finally, everyone at Ecotricity, past and present. What we've done was team work.